Networking for the Novice, Nervous, or Naïve Job Seeker

The advice is consistent –
Networking is key to any job search!

The statistics are encouraging—nearly 80 percent of job openings are never advertised and more than two thirds of candidates get a job through networking. The bottom line is discouraging—the majority of job seekers spend most of their job-search time sitting at their computer navigating through various employment sites and responding to advertised openings.

Why?

In a nutshell—fear: fear of rejection, fear of the unknown, and fear of trying things out of their normal comfort zone. Combine that with a lack of understanding of how networking works during the hiring process and it becomes easy to see why the job candidate finds a greater comfort level behind his or her computer screen.

But, this strategy only exposes him or her to a limited number of opportunities, and since all job seekers use the classifieds and job boards, they face the highest level of competition.

The best news of all is that you can benefit from networking during your job search. Networking can provide the foundation for your job search, support each area of your search, and also provide you with opportunities to expand your horizons throughout your career.

Networking for the Novice, Nervous, or Naïve Job Seeker

Tom Dezell

iUniverse, Inc.
New York   Bloomington

iUniverse books may be ordered through booksellers or by contacting:

iUniverse
1663 Liberty Drive
Bloomington, IN 47403
www.iuniverse.com
1-800-Authors (1-800-288-4677)

Because of the dynamic nature of the Internet, any Web addresses or links contained in this book may have changed since publication and may no longer be valid. The views expressed in this work are solely those of the author and do not necessarily reflect the views of the publisher, and the publisher hereby disclaims any responsibility for them.

ISBN: 978-1-4401-6609-9 (sc)
ISBN: 978-1-4401-6610-5 (ebook)
ISBN: 978-1-4401-6611-2 (dj)

Library of Congress Control Number: 2009933827

Printed in the United States of America

iUniverse rev. date: 9/28/2009

Acknowledgements

Thanks to Nancy Fink and Steve Gallison for selecting me for the POAC team and sharing all their knowledge with me over the years. Also, to John Shea, Matt Hein and Barb Lovitts for reviewing my initial draft. I wouldn't have had the courage to forge ahead without your candid feedback. Special thanks on the cover and marketing reviews to Mark Feldman, Asa Williams and Lauren Thompson.

To my sister, Maureen Dezell, for guiding me through the author process and suggesting the title. To my sons, Eric and Kevin, for who both of you are and what you mean to me. Finally, to Mom. I know you're proud to have a second author in your stable, but miss being able to sign your copy.

Table of Contents

Chapter 1

Employment Networking—An Overview

Your reaction to the word "networking" will vary greatly depending on your chosen profession. If you work in sales, marketing, politics, or development, the term should be familiar. Success in these fields requires one to continuously build and maintain strong networking ties to fortify a base of clients, customers, voters, or donors. You may also use it to varying degrees of success if you participate in network level marketing. Oddly, even though people in these areas recognize the need to network in their everyday business, they do not always realize the importance of networking when they search for a new job or career.

Many of the rest of us do not necessarily need to consistently build and maintain a network as part of our chosen profession. We only face the prospect of networking when we begin one of the most arduous tasks we will ever undertake—the search for employment.

A novice, nervous, or naïve job seeker might enter the job search process in the form of:

- A new college graduate entering the big, bad job market for the first time
- A recently downsized financial professional thrust into the job search
- A stay-at-home parent reentering the workforce
- A mid-level manager whose company either shut down or moved operations elsewhere

These are only a handful of the countless scenarios in which people face the prospect of searching for employment. More often than we would like, we reach this status unexpectedly or with feelings of disappointment. Our current position may no longer fill our needs. We do not play a part in our employer's plans anymore. Our position was shipped overseas. The reasons can be numerous.

Searching for a job ranks right along with root canal work on the desired activity scale of the average human being. For this reason, many delay beginning their job search longer than they should, hoping (springing eternally) that their tenuous situation will change for the better. Unfortunately, once you lose your job, you now face that dreaded task of searching for a new job—a process labeled by my friend and colleague, Steve Gallison, as the "job acquisition process." The process will have this moniker throughout this book.

Typically, job seekers begin by pouring themselves into the world of Internet job boards and newspaper classifieds. A very small minority finds quick luck here. The vast majority receives marginal to no results at all. Slowly they realize that one to two interviews per month will not ultimately result in a quick placement.

Struggling, they pick up some of the many excellent how-to books on job search and also attend seminars on the same subject. As they become more informed, they hear the startling statistics about the success rates of their main job search methods. When I first read *What Color is your Parachute* in 1980, I learned the stark reality about the problems with strictly relying on advertised openings. In the latest version of *Parachute*, Boles indicates that only five to twenty-four percent of job seekers find success in answering newspaper ads.[1] That number has remained constant throughout my career. The data on Internet job boards is still in its infancy, and I could inundate you with additional statistical data from various other sources, but rarely do the numbers increase. The novice, nervous, and naïve job seekers at this point realize that the methods they currently use will only expose them to a small percentage of available jobs.

As they attempt to tap into the hidden job market, or the job openings that aren't advertised, the job seeker realizes the truth in the catchphrase, "It's not *what* you know, but *who* you know." For some job seekers discovering this means just a simple change in strategy.

They begin researching their own networks, jump online and on the telephone, and begin making contacts. It seems very natural to them.

However, many job seekers become queasy about this prospect. These are the people who often describe themselves with terms like "private," "introvert," or "non-sales person." The prospect of contacting any person outside of their immediate comfort circle, let alone dozens, overwhelms them with anxiety. Rather than trying to analyze and overcome their fears, many such job seekers decide to spend more hours on their computers under the comfort of anonymity. With more than one hundred thousand career related Web sites to choose from, in addition to all the companies with links for online applications, the job seeker can accrue countless hours of job search time on the Internet. While this strategy constitutes working hard at finding a job, the data clearly shows it fails to pass the test of working smart. Most likely, the length of their search for work continuously increases.

I know all these feelings very well because I have been there. While no friends, colleagues, or acquaintances have ever described me as private or introverted, career-based personality tests never encourage me to enter the sales field. I rank very low on assertiveness scores, and often they are my lowest scores.

My most eye-opening reality check in this area occurred in my final year at Northeastern University. In their fine College of Criminal Justice, I studied under Professor Spencer Rathus, author of the *Rathus Assertiveness Scale*. Since the survey was part of his course curriculum, I happily completed one. My score placed me in the lowest two percent of males. I knew I was not entering the sales field, but as a soon-to-be graduate, I was concerned about such a low score. I noted this would be an area to monitor early in my career.

Unfortunately, my initial jobs enabled me to hide this weakness rather than confront it. I never really had to build a network. Most of my interactions with others came in very controlled settings. I spent seven years as a caseworker in correctional programs—about as controlled a setting as you can get. I never had to reach out for clients; they *had* to talk to me.

The correctional facilities operated as work release programs.

I quickly discovered that I enjoyed the career development aspects of my casework the most. I learned how to effectively work with employers to hire the offenders on my caseload. While developing a placement rate that I became proud of, I began to appreciate the importance a person's job and career play in his or her life. I also discovered how rewarding it was to assist in locating, even in a very small way, a job for a client. Steve Gallison coined another great term about this. He says he cashes a psychic check whenever a client finds work.

Like many people a few years into their career, I began to question whether the corrections field, with all its baggage, could sustain my interest for the rest of my working life. Job placement proved to be my most transferable skill. I marketed my record in job development for "unique" or "difficult" populations. This lead to two new jobs with increased networking requirements.

I was hired as the employment coordinator for a welfare-to-work clerical training program and I needed to drum up large volumes of job orders. With a program goal of thirty placements per class, I quickly discovered that reaching this number would involve scheduling two hundred or more interviews per group. This forced me to contact people through many different avenues and work up job leads. The program had a base of contacts when I started, so I was not totally out in the cold. But as anyone in the field of job placement can attest, contacts at companies change quite often. Building and re-establishing new leads required ongoing assertive networking.

I performed this successfully enough to land my next and most challenging job to date: placement of injured workers receiving workers compensation. Five years in this environment required my networking, contacts and closing skills to grow exponentially. I did not have the strength of a previously established employer base or the reputation of the training program to support me. Placement generally resulted from intensive one-on-one contacts. Unfortunately for the company, the caseworkers, and the clients I worked for, much of my growth came with me kicking and screaming the entire way, as I greatly resisted expanding my contact comfort zone for a long time. However, by the time I left this field, I could contact and talk to people in manners and situations I had never imagined.

I conduct countless job acquisition seminars a year now. Having seen hundreds of job seekers ranging from the convicted felon to the six-figure executive obtain employment, I stress to job seekers that a networking lead will be the initial source of contact with a new employer at least fifty percent of the time. This has been demonstrated not only by research data, but by the actual results I have seen in more than twenty-five years of work in job acquisition.

My teaching style uses real-life stories derived from previous job candidates to illustrate points. As I describe stories of successful networking leads and continually emphasize the need to network, I regularly see a certain look in the eyes of many job seekers—the look of fear and discomfort. I can tell how instinctively uncomfortable they feel about the prospect of engaging in interpersonal interactions so foreign to their normal interpersonal styles. That look in their eyes also reflects a double stress for them. Not only do they face one of the most difficult jobs in our economy—finding a job—they now realize that doing so may also require learning to use personality traits they have never had to develop. They do not know if they can sufficiently develop these skills on the fly in order to succeed in job acquisition.

I know exactly what the fears in every pair of eyes are. I understand them because I have, at one point in my career, experienced every one of those fears. Typically, most of the people preaching the need to network to you are those to whom networking comes naturally. They may not be a great source of any remedial techniques to assist you. I offer the perspective of someone who once ranked in the lowest two percent on an assertiveness scale. I improved enough over time to successfully facilitate job placement activities for three extremely difficult populations. My need to succeed forced me to confront my fears and become a networker. This was not an overnight transition and it will not be for anyone else who needs to upgrade their networking skills. However, I firmly believe that if I can make the leap from where I began to where I am now as a networker, anyone else can improve also. While your primary need to improve your network right now may involve a current job search or new career venture, you will find that maintaining these skills will enhance both your personal and professional lives. This will make later career moves and changes much easier. Also, you may reap the tremendous satisfaction of providing network assistance to a contact and help them further his or her goals.

If you want improvement in anything, you must first commit to making change. Start out with this commitment toward improving your networking. Each day, resolve yourself to *make at least two contacts that are beyond your normal comfort range.* Practice this over and over and, in time, your range of comfort will expand to heights you never imagined. You also will develop much stronger interpersonal skills and enhance your job interviewing abilities. Each will be a great asset to your short-term job acquisition needs as well as long-term career goals.

You will see many references and analogies to sales techniques throughout this book. Like it or not, job acquisition is a sales process, with candidates "selling" their talents and abilities to "buyers," or employers. Unless you work in the sales field, you most likely have had limited, if any, sales training. I strongly recommend reading sales training books such as *The Sales Bible: The Ultimate Sales Resource* by Jeffrey Gitomer and *Knock Your Socks Off Selling* by Jeffrey Gitomer and Ron Zemke. I realize that with little to no sales background, the techniques described in these books could easily overwhelm you. If this is the case, try reading the books with the following philosophy: For every ten strategies or techniques the authors recommend, find one or two you would feel comfortable trying. Test them out. Once you develop comfort in these, move on to some others with increased levels of assertiveness.

Three particular areas you should read up on and consult with business-to-business sales professionals about, include:

- Discovering the "decision maker" of a company. This is the primary individual a sales representative wants to approach. Job seekers need to approach an employer the same way. What employee within a company would ultimately decide whether to hire you or not? This is the individual you want to market your talents to.
- Methods of overcoming barriers faced in reaching decision makers, such as phone screenings and voicemail. Learn how sales professionals persist in their sales goals.

- Networking tips. Learn as many as possible from books about sales and discussions with sales professionals. Just as with any sales tips you learn, listen and start only with the methods you feel comfortable with. Add additional methods to your repertoire as you master the initial ones.

An additional resource I recommend is the Web site Businessbyphone.com. The majority of your contacts will be via telephone. This site is geared for telephone sales professionals and contains valuable information on improving telephone contact techniques.

Every job search book contains statistics on how jobs are filled. The numbers of jobs obtained through networking range from fifty to eighty percent depending on the source. There are many reasons why so many jobs end up being filled by network contacts. I will attempt to address most of these in the next chapter. Then I will look at common reasons, excuses, and misconceptions that hinder many job seekers from networking. I'll show you why these beliefs are often fallacious and unfounded so that, hopefully, you will overcome some of your own objections to networking. Once this is out of the way, we will look at strategies to get your networking started. Tips and anecdotes will appear throughout, and I'll close with some select real-life examples.

Throughout the book, the text in bold gives useful tips about networking or job searches.

Chapter 2

Why Networking is So Important to the Job Acquisition Process

Many job seekers struggle with the concept of the hidden job market. They ponder why employers only advertise openings twenty percent of the time. Why can't they access all available jobs? They ask, "How can I find out who's hiring?" and "Why does it have to be who you know, not what you know?"

Most of the complaints about the hidden job market grow out of a basic lack of understanding about how the hiring process works. Job seekers fail to realize that most employers find other methods of finding candidates more effective than advertising on boards or in newspapers. From all my years of job and career development, I believe one of the most consistent mistakes job seekers make is never considering the hiring process *from the employer's point of view*. Even those who have made hiring decisions throughout their own careers often fail to view the process from the other side of the desk in their own search.

Starting with the basics, any employer looking to fill a position has a need. The need escalates to the problem level the longer the position remains unfilled. When looking to fill the position, the hiring manager will seek:

- The candidate with the best skills and abilities to solve the problems that created the opening.

- The candidate who will be best suited to deal with the problems as quickly as possible.
- An individual who will fit in and work effectively with the existing staff.

Once a hiring manager needs to fill a position, she will likely take the following steps, in varying order:

- Consider candidates she already knows meeting the above criteria, including former colleagues and associates she has developed relationships with throughout her career.
- Reach out to her professional network to inquire about strong potential candidates. Recommendations of fellow professionals the manager respects provide assurances of a candidate's capabilities to perform the job.
- Consult with current employees for potential referrals.

Anytime I meet a high level human resource professional from any size company, one of my first questions is "What percentage of your jobs are filled through referrals from current employees?" If they track such statistics, the answers will amaze you. I have never heard an answer of less than twenty percent and have heard as high as fifty-five percent. At various times in my career, three of the largest employers in the Baltimore metro area have quoted percentages of forty-five, fifty, and fifty-five percent respectively.

Because of this, many companies have incentive programs that offer cash rewards for successful referrals of hired employees, provided the new hire remains on the job a minimum, predetermined amount of time. This trend continues to grow. Even employers without incentives recognize the power of internal referrals. Any employee who values his or her standing within companies will only refer strong candidates. This is especially true if the employee will work closely with the new hire. An existing relationship with a current employee allows the candidate to have:

- A greater awareness of what problems the candidate expects to face and solve.

- An idea of the company culture and how to fit in.

When employers evaluate various methods used to recruit job candidates, you can see why people known to either the hiring manager or current employees often develop into both stronger candidates and potentially better employees than those recruited via other methods. They enter the recruitment process with a better knowledge of the job, the company culture, and the hiring preferences of the hiring manager. Adding to the incentive for the employer can be the relatively low cost of such a hire. Even without such a formal incentive referral policy, companies that track their hiring sources will often discover that most of their top employees come from this method.

For comparison purposes, let's examine various hiring scenarios and explore the pros and cons of each.

Recruitment Option A
The candidate is known by either the hiring manager or through an employee referral (including a candidate the manager knows will have interest).

This offers advantages, including expediency—candidates can be presented and qualified quickly. The employer understands that the candidate has some knowledge of the company in terms of policies and mission. With such knowledge, the candidate only pursues the job if she or he has a definite interest. Training time is at least shortened, and sometimes almost eliminated, due to the candidate's familiarity. Such scenarios mean the least loss of production time.

Should no such candidates surface through the referral method, the employer can start to attempt the following recruitment methods. The first are "free" only in terms that no invoice is sent to an employer. They may not be free in terms of staff time.

Recruitment Option B
Posting the opening in public.

This produces the best results at large employers or ones with high visibility. People know that to find out if company X is hiring, they either visit the company Web site or go there in person to check their notices. Such well-known employers rarely suffer from a lack of applicants. They face potential downfalls, though. Depending on the age of the application, the status of the candidates can be uncertain. Many strong candidates could no longer be in the job market.

Job seekers often fail to realize the strain that processing high volumes of résumés and or applications puts on employers. The staff hours required to review and qualify these documents can be staggering, making a known or referred candidate preferable to any type of outside posting. If the known candidate's credentials meet the job requirements and the hiring party believes in their capabilities to do the job, most employers will extend a job offer and save the time and money which comes along with any search involving high volumes of applications or résumés to review.

As the volume of applications increases, chances increase that the initial review will be delegated to a human resource office, clerical staff, or even possibly sent out to an agency. While these strategies often involve highly competent people, they increasingly become more removed from the scope of the actual job parameters. They rely on written instructions and criteria from hiring managers to screen. This can lead to more "vanilla" candidates, as the reviewers cannot pick up as many "soft" skills or intangibles a reviewer closer to the job site could discover. Similarly, phone screening candidates can produce similar results. The farther away the screener is from the actual job responsibilities, the greater the chance for strong candidates "slipping through the cracks." I realize many strong employees have been hired through these methods, but the success rates may not be as high as that of referred candidates.

Recruitment Option C
Free listing services in government employment offices.
This provides the employer large pools of potential candidates as well as free uploading to certain national Internet job banks. Staff at one-stop career centers will "screen" candidates for the employer. While this reduces lost staff time and costs to the employers, these screeners sit far removed from not only the job duties but also the company culture. One-stop staff may have to screen for hundreds of employers. Additionally, the centers often offer a well-intentioned

policy of limiting the number of referrals. This can easily turn into a "first come-first served" referral basis. Better, more qualified candidates that inquire about the job opening may see only a closed door.

Recruitment Option D
List the opening with placement offices at schools, colleges, or trade institutions.

Specialized training institutions offer the employer the advantage of qualifying candidates by people knowledgeable in the field of specialization. While this will make the quality of referrals stronger from these sources, they often only offer candidates for entry-level positions. Mid-to-upper level positions can rarely be filled in this manner.

College placement offices face some of the same dilemmas a government placement office has in terms of screening candidates. They try to serve a large base of employers, so preparing candidates for the needs of a particular company end up falling on the employer themselves. Plus, recent college graduates only qualify for select, mostly entry-level positions. Employers with needs in mid-to-upper-level areas can't use these services very well, unless it's a job fair.

Tip

Mid- and upper-level candidates have found success attending college job fairs. The setting allows for potential face-to-face meetings with key individuals at desired companies. While the company may only recruit for more entry-level positions at such a fair, other openings may exist or become available shortly thereafter.

Recruitment Option E
Advertise the vacant position.

If employers try and cannot find quality candidates from the cost-free methods, they must now absorb the cost of advertising for openings. Many candidates blame the fact that so few jobs are available as indicative of discrimination or the "good ol' boy network" working again. I will not pretend this does not exist, but more often the reason for the lack of advertisement is much more a reflection of all the costs involved, which I outlined above.

To reach the largest pool of local candidates, ads are posted in Sunday editions of major newspapers. Rates vary by circulation and part of the country, but the ads come with a significant price tag. Smaller companies struggle with this much more than larger companies. Posting on major job boards presents the same problem. To get an idea of these costs, go to any job board and click on the link for "new employers" or "post a job opening" to see what costs employers face.

Not only does the cost of advertising cripple a small business, but we've already documented how processing hundreds of paper or electronically submitted résumés places serious time burdens on the existing staff. Think of how many staffers wear multiple hats in a small business. How eager are they to add such a task to their daily to do lists?

As I outline these cost factors incurred by smaller companies, bear in mind that the Small Business Administration Office of Advocacy reports that small businesses have generated sixty to eighty percent of net new jobs annually over the last decade in the United States (www.sba.gov Frequently Asked Questions-How important are small businesses to the U. S. Economy).

Larger companies can handle volume better, but as stated earlier, they often rely on techniques conducted by staff and technology further removed from the job's actual operations. This can be especially true when HR functions are "outsourced." Scanning résumés and applications into databases makes processing easier, but this makes keywords in the résumé vital. While it may make screening résumés more efficient, have the top candidates always ended up being hired?

This is a cursory view of potential steps employers take to fill open positions. Once they've tried each of these, many employers review their recruiting methods. They may evaluate their current staff and determine what sources brought each staff member in. Based on many of the pitfalls of other methods mentioned above, it can be easy to see why referred candidates often become the most successful employees. Thus, this becomes a preferred method of recruiting. As a result, many companies will place a higher priority on developing incentives, some of which are financial, designed to encourage internal referrals.

Here is a brief sampling of some company policies just in my local area:

- A recruiter from one of Baltimore's largest financial firms spoke to a networking group of unemployed professionals and indicated that forty-five percent of their hires come from employee referrals, and told the group that they maintain all referred résumés in a database. Stressing how beneficial an internal referral can be, the recruiter pointed out that once an employee drops off a résumé, HR can check and see that the candidate has already sent them a résumé previously. Many have responded to numerous openings. Even if no previous submission had resulted in the candidate making the interview list, now having "employee referral" status would likely get the candidate at least a telephone interview.

- One top-twenty employer in the county where I work offers a $3,000 cash bonus to employees that refer a candidate that is hired and remains more than ninety days. "Referred" résumés will also automatically be routed to the hiring manager in addition to human resources. All other résumés are screened by the human resource department prior to referral to the hiring manager.

- I once had a customer target this company for a finance position and send me his application package for critiquing. Knowing how this company policy on "referred" status, I contacted a former customer working there to see if she would refer him. She happily did and they proceeded to correspond a couple of times via e-mail. He interviewed, and received and accepted a job offer. To the surprise of the human resource representative introducing him around his first day, they did not immediately recognize each other. Only after identifying him as her referral did they realize their connection. Yes, she still received her bonus.

I constantly repeat this story to those job seekers highly engaged in the seemingly endless maze of posting or mailing résumés to larger companies. They often lament, "If I could just talk with someone inside to sell my skills." Well, now you know of a potential way to make this happen: find an inside referral.

I hope this has provided a better understanding as to why employers benefit from networked candidates. Now we will examine how networking assists applicants. Some are obvious, but many are factors that job seekers do not fully realize or fail to understand. The bottom line remains that networking provides the job seeker many opportunities to become a stronger candidate.

Networking can relieve the anxiety of an introvert.

Many people who lack networking skills describe themselves as shy or introverted. The job acquisition process presents an extra challenge for these personality types. Steve Gallison (I will quote him quite often throughout the book) is the Director of Maryland's Professional Outplacement Assistance Center (POAC) where I work. He stresses in every seminar that the job acquisition process favors highly verbal candidates. This makes sense with interviewing and networking being so critical to landing a job offer. The extensive amount of contacting and meeting so many new people could stress even many extroverts. An introvert could end up requiring medication.

Many introverts with whom I have worked throughout my career say that using networked leads can *reduce* their anxiety level. The reason is that if an employer already knows something about them via a third party, the candidate will have less to explain about himself or herself in a meeting or interview. This knowledge can relieve much of the anxiety the candidate experiences. The dreaded opening question of "tell me about yourself" becomes less daunting. Any job seeker can understand how much more relaxed he or she becomes in an interview once their top stress-producing issue is eliminated. By and large, a more relaxed candidate will interview much better than an anxious one.

Having placed ex-offenders and injured workers, I can truly attest to how much better these candidates performed on interviews I had arranged for them. If I had referred them to a particular employer, they *knew* the hiring manager was aware of their "issue" or "barrier" and would not immediately disqualify them. It was amazing how much better they performed in these interviews as opposed to ones where they had to explain every barrier on their own.

Networked candidates have greater access to information about the company and the hiring managers. This makes for a better informed candidate able to interview with better awareness of the employer's needs.

We all know the cliché, "knowledge is power." If properly used, a network lead can provide a candidate with insight into the mindset of the hiring authority. Let's start at the beginning with submitting résumés for review. Hiring managers regularly report that the résumés with the most impact are ones that speak to their individual needs. Sadly, most résumé senders either never consider this or find the task of customizing each résumé to the desires of particular employers too cumbersome. What many fail to realize is that any referral source can possibly provide the candidate valuable insight into the priorities of the hiring manager.

Let me present the following scenario. A local company of 110 employees has a need for a graphic designer. They post an ad in the local paper. Upon seeing the ad, one candidate remembers that a member of her religious congregation works for the company, though not in the graphics department. Still, she expresses interest to her contact, who promises to investigate the opening. The contact asks some fellow employees about the graphics design department and how it functions. In their conversation, it is revealed that the opening occurred due to the termination of an employee for repeated missed deadlines and exceeding budgets. Once this information is relayed to the candidate, she adds or highlights a bullet to each job indicating her track record of meeting ninety-nine percent of her deadlines and never exceeding budget. Do you think this résumé may impress that hiring manager more than one with no reference to such information? Absolutely!

Many job seekers fail to realize how easily information like this can be obtained by an existing employee, no matter what department he or she works in. A few questions to the right people can elicit such information very quickly. In the case we discussed, word of a termination travels through company grapevines very quickly. Yet countless candidates with contacts employed at companies where they apply to fail to ask any questions when they are a candidate. (We will address many of the reasons why later.)

Tip

As a Certified Professional Résumé Writer (CPRW), I know that tailoring one's résumé to the individual needs of a particular employer is one of the most effective ways to create interest from an employer. It drives me crazy when candidates fail to use possible networking information to enhance the résumés they send. Even when either an employee or the hiring manager has provided the candidate with information regarding the pending projects, skill preferences, or simple style, candidates still send their generic, "one-size-fits-all" résumé. Prior to sending any individual your résumé, ask what you know about that individual, their job, or the company. Look at your résumé and see if there's any way you can improve the résumé to reflect those needs.

Many candidates believe that customizing each résumé is synonymous with re-writing each résumé. No! Customizing is about adjusting. If you use a qualifications or career summary, adjust it to particulars of the job, much like you rewrite cover letters. Stronger emphasis of select skills, achievements, or accomplishments can make a big difference in catching a certain reader's attention. Review the bullet phrases you list for each position. You do not have to present them in the same sequence for all employers. One achievement you describe around the fourth or fifth bullet of your résumé may relate directly to a project the hiring company has just begun. If you find this out, list that bullet first on the résumé you send them.

Your chances to enhance your candidacy with unearthed tidbits of information are endless. Imagine a candidate who for the past ten years has left any reference off his résumé to his years of service in the United States Marines. He discovers, through a contact, that the hiring manager for a job he wants to apply for also served in the Marines. I would strongly recommend that this candidate include their Marines experience in the résumé they send for this position.

One of my favorite career columnists, Penelope Trunk, otherwise known as the Brazen Careerist, could not put this reality any more succinctly:

> **Hiring managers do not hire the most qualified person: They hire the individual they most want to work with. Whether this is fair is not up for discussion, because the philosophical and de facto practices of corporate hiring are not going to change anytime soon.[2]**

I would add that this applies to any employer, not just corporations. A factor in determining with whom hiring managers most want to work can be shared backgrounds and experiences. This is why I would recommend the candidate add the Marines to this résumé. The idea of a fellow Marine on staff may resonate with this particular employer. Thus, including it on the résumé, as opposed to a summary of college coursework, would make the candidate more appealing.

Good networking does not only apply to making your résumé more marketable to the company or hiring manager. Nor does it stop once an interview is scheduled. A candidate can use such information to enhance any contact with an employer, ranging from a brief contact at a business mixer all the way through telephone screenings and job interviews.

You are interviewing any time you have contact with an employee or representative of a company you are interested in.

The initial minutes of any employment contact usually decide whether you become a candidate for hire or not. As Dale Carnegie says, "So the only way on earth to influence other people is to talk about what they want and how to get it."[3] So if you have some prior knowledge of what an employer wants and how you can help them get it, this increases your rapport with the employer from the beginning. Networking with the right people can provide a great source of information on the needs and interests of key decision makers who you contact in your job search.

Can you now see why networked candidates often interview better? If they have obtained information about specific needs, projects, or issues facing the hiring manager, they can address their ability to handle these right from the beginning. A less informed candidate needs to probe in the interview to determine this. In a sports analogy, would you rather play a big game with a scouting report on your opponent or feel him or her out and adjust during the contest?

Closing out this theme, I will cite an example of how networking can even help *after* you receive a job offer. Remember, once an offer is received, you will need to negotiate your compensation package. If you have ever negotiated anything (like car or home prices), you certainly have learned that knowledge is power. The story of a job seeker I worked with illustrates this point precisely.

The case involves a systems analyst hit hard by the fallout in the information technology field during the recession of 2001 to 2004. After seven to eight months of trying to locate work in the DC metro area failed to gain a job offer, he decided he must consider relocation in his job search. An old colleague who had moved to Dallas, Texas several years earlier eagerly presented the job seekers résumé to his superiors. They liked that he had experience in the type of federal government contracts similar to ones recently awarded to the company. After a series of interviews, he got an offer, ending his nine-month ordeal.

The new company offered a generous salary and a couple of thousand dollars toward relocation. This was helpful but would not cover all of his moving expenses. The weakest part of the offer stemmed from the policy that health insurance would not be available to a new hire until after six months of service. The man had a child with special medical needs, and he had been carrying $1,100 per month of COBRA payments since leaving his last job.

Having recently read Ron Shapiro's book *The Power of Nice*, he remembered Shapiro's emphasis on offering a win-win approach to negotiations. During the initial referral period, his colleague had told him the company had been struggling to fill this job for over four months at the time he first interviewed. This made the total lapse in the position five months by the time he started. Based on the concepts from the Shapiro book, the candidate made the following proposal to his new employer:

I am very happy with the position offered and the salary. My only area of concern is that I will need to wait six months to join the company's health insurance plan and understand there is no flexibility in that date. I currently carry a $1,100 per month COBRA payment, which will prove quite burdensome for six more months. Since my position was vacant for five months, I recognize that the department's budget has saved over twenty-five thousand dollars during that period. From these savings, could the company possibly pay my COBRA until I'm on the health plan?

The company agreed. While a great deal of credit goes to the candidate for his win-win negotiation, think of how vital to his request the knowledge of the length of the opening was. He received that information from his contact. Information is often there, but many do not use it.

Hopefully, this information has helped you—the novice, nervous, or naïve job seeker—better understand some of the many benefits networking can provide during your period of job acquisition. Good networking is not just a good ol' boy system at work. It is a mutually beneficial process between job candidates and employers. Even when jobs open through advertised channels, good networking can improve one's chances at receiving a job offer and negotiating a compensation package.

Even with this understanding, many candidates remain reluctant to increase their networking activity. In our next chapter, we will examine many of the common reasons job seekers choose either to not network or only do so on a limited basis.

Chapter 3

Networking Misconceptions

In the final years of both high school and college, I took courses that introduced me to concepts I have found very practical in the counseling and advising roles of my career. In the first semester of my senior year of high school at Loyola High of Baltimore—a fine Jesuit institution—I took a course designed to train us how to write college term papers. We spent the entire first half of the course dealing with the common mistakes and fallacies associated with the thesis statement. Our teacher, Mr. Tim Pierce, stressed that writing a strong paper becomes nearly impossible if the thesis statement is illogical or based on a fallacy.

In my senior year at Northeastern University's College of Criminal Justice, I took courses in theories of counseling taught by my friend Professor Rathus and developed an appreciation for Dr. Albert Ellis's Rational Emotive Behavior Therapy (REBT). To paraphrase Dr. Ellis, adherence to irrational, self-defeating beliefs is the actual source of much individual unhappiness. By identifying these beliefs and allowing the patient to realize how false or unattainable the thoughts are, successful therapy could ensue.

I bring these concepts up because I have learned through my years in career development that job seekers usually fail to network enough because they hold erroneous beliefs about networking. Even when confronted with all the facts about the percentage of jobs filled through networking, many job seekers continue to talk themselves out of increasing their network contacts. If you are a job seeker and accept the reality that sixty percent or more of jobs are located via networking, ask yourself this question: Do you spend over sixty percent of your job acquisition time engaged in networking activities? Most job seekers I deal with admit their own ratio is not even close. Sadly, their reasons for not networking often mirror the problems created by a bad thesis statement or an erroneous belief system. The job seeker has developed concepts about networking that are either misguided or just plain false. I want to reference three views on this subject:

- Jeff Gitomer, author of *The Sales Bible: The Ultimate Sales Resource,* warns sales professionals of the dangers of missing opportunities by focusing too much on obstacles. "If you focus on the negative, the results will likely be negative. If you focus on positive anticipation and positive outcome, then positive results will follow."[4]

- In his book *The Unwritten Rules of a Highly Effective Job Search: The Proven Program Used by the World's Leading Career Services Firm,* Oliver Pierson compares job acquisition to hunting. Mr. Pierson notes that "… in job search, the animals to watch out for aren't in the woods. They're inside you. In your mind. The biggest obstacles to success are the inner beasts: fear, feeling worthless, lacking confidence, and many others."[5] Since Mr. Pierson designs a job search program effectively used by more than one hundred thousand job seekers per year, I believe he has strong insight into the mindset of most job seekers.

- Cornerstone Executive Life & Coaching quotes nationally known speaker Collette Carlson on their Web site, Excetutive-and-Life-Coaching.com, when discussing enemies within us. "Therefore the first step to fighting the enemy within is to be aware that there is an enemy and that he is not looking out for your best interests. He is telling you lies. Colette Carlson calls them LIES, which stands for Limiting Ideas Eliminate Success."

The following chapters will look at many of the self-limiting misconceptions about networking I have heard in the course of my career, and attempt to demonstrate their lack of validity. (These misconceptions result in many of the obstacles Pierson mentions.) Hopefully this will eliminate many self-imposed barriers to the networking process and make your own job acquisition process more fruitful.

Chapter 4

The Novice Job Seeker

Self-Limiting Misconception Number One: I anticipate a short job search. I will not start networking unless the search takes longer than anticipated.

While this may not be the most prevalent belief blocking the network process, I address it first as it can be the easiest to slip into.

The first problem is that establishing or reestablishing your network takes time, so it is imperative to begin networking as soon as you enter the job acquisition process. In making networking contacts, you will need to allow time for them to develop. Some contacts may need to check with some of their connections; others may provide you with contacts for you to follow up with on your own.

I will outline specific network strategies later in the book. One major concept to stress is the need to focus network contacts on providing career advice. This will open doors to all potential sources your contact may have. All too often, a job seeker only asks a contact about job openings at his or her place of employment. When that is the only information requested, that will be the only information received. Dick Gaither, director of Job Search Training Systems, Inc., ranks this as number three in his list of twenty-seven common job search mistakes. Gaither believes the most destructive words in a job seeker's vocabulary are the opening questions "Are you hiring?" or "Do you have any jobs?" He reasons that this opens up the contact in a manner likely to result in a negative answer.

Many novice networkers delay networking under the false

hope that they will find something quickly. Unfortunately, once the classifieds and job boards have yielded limited results, they *then* feel the pressure to start networking. Under duress, they engage in what Diane Darling, president of Effective Networking, Inc., calls "911 Networking." They make their focus only contacts with potential immediate openings, which does not utilize the full power of network referrals. Once this strategy fails to produce immediate results, they sour on the networking process. While the frustration is understandable, the result will often be a longer job search period and an even more frustrated and discouraged job seeker. That, sadly, can become a vicious cycle.

The second big problem with this strategy is that anticipating a short job search might be akin to waiting for the tooth fairy. I had previously referenced Dick Gaither's list of the twenty-seven most common job search mistakes. Gaither ranks *underestimating the competitive nature of a job search* as the number one mistake. If your last job search occurred during particularly robust economic times, such as the booms of the 1980s and mid to late 1990s, you may have found new jobs very quickly. Well, 2009 is a different ballgame. During those boom periods, the economy created jobs faster than workers became available to fill them—hence, the hiring occurred at a record pace. A reflection of this is that during the boom of the 1980s, the fastest growing service industry was search firms. They grew in the '90s as well, but not at as brisk a pace; search firms had become more established by then.

The labor market since the 2000s has behaved in different ways than before. During the rebound from the recession of the early years of the decade, the slowest area to get back on track was hiring. The term "jobless recovery" became a popular explanation of the employment figures lagging behind other strong economic figures. Even while general job statistics have improved, a recent CNN Money report revealed an interesting statistic. The percentage of workers who remain unemployed in excess of twenty-six weeks grew from eleven percent in 2000 to 17.6 percent in 2007. The labor market downturn commencing in 2008 promises to increase this trend.

Another factor to consider is a general change in the nature of the hiring process. Corporate scandals and 9/11 resulted in increased scrutiny of the background investigations of employment candidates. Factors such as these contribute to slowing down the hiring process, adding more time to many job searches.

Kate Wendleton is a nationally-syndicated speaker and columnist and the president of the Five O'Clock Club, a national networking organization. She probably has as accurate a picture of the labor market as anyone in the country. In an article by Carrie Mason-Draffen in the *Baltimore Sun* on August 31, 2005, Mason-Draffen quotes Kate Wendleton as saying, "We want our job hunters to have six to ten strong job possibilities at any one time. They need this because five to seven of the leads will fail to develop through no fault of the job seeker." Any job seeker needs to ask himself, how long will it take to develop that many strong leads? Also, do you believe you can develop that volume of leads via classified ads and job boards?

A final factor to consider is that as you move up in your career, the average length of the job search will increase as a result of your success. Outplacement professionals often quote another "rule of thumb" to employment candidates: *For every ten thousand in salary of the job you seek, figure about one month of average search time.* So for a forty-thousand-dollar position, the search may average four months. A search for a seventy-thousand-dollar position could last more than half a year.

I have followed sports my whole life, which has made me a statistical geek, so I love to check out statistics such as this for validity. I recently had access to some return-to-work figures for a group of dislocated professionals participating in Department of Labor funded programs. I surveyed a group of nearly five hundred returns-to-work from 2000 to 2004. The average annual salary of the group's new jobs was $58,500. The average search time was 6.5 months. There were plenty of individual disparities, and the average remained in the six- to seven-month range for the workers who earned seventy thousand dollars and above. However, the overall data supports this "rule of thumb." Higher paying jobs come open less frequently, the competition is more intense, and they are more likely to be filled through networking leads. It only follows that finding such jobs will take longer. As you progress in your career, you'll command a higher salary and qualify for more responsible positions.

So remember, if you've been lucky enough to have brief job searches in the past and had to network very little, labor market experts say, and statistics show, this trend is unlikely to continue. The best way to shorten a job search is to make use of all resources available to finding potential openings.

Tip

If you begin a new job search with a severance package, avoid the temptation that can lead to what I term "Severance Sloth." When receiving either continued paychecks or a lump sum covering a set period of time, it becomes tempting to use your newfound free time as a brief vacation. The problem comes when that vacation mindset puts the job search into a cruise control mindset. In this mode the job seeker often delays or avoids the more difficult parts of job search; targeting companies, assessing skills, planning strategies, and developing or contacting network lists. Keep the following factors in mind if you hope to start out slowly:

- **Will the more difficult tasks you avoid become any easier once the severance money runs out?**
- **Do you feel better marketing and selling your talent with added financial stress?**
- **What evidence do you see that the labor market will improve right around the time your severance package expires?**

I will finish this misconception with an analogy. You decide to go fishing on vacation. The area has five lakes available for fishing. The local fishing store shows you the results of surveys it has done with people after fishing in each of the five lakes. One lake boasts a catch rate of fifty-five percent. The other four report rates of sixteen percent, twelve percent, nine percent, and eight percent respectively. Which lake do *you* want to fish in?

Self-Limiting Misconception Number Two: I know a contact within a company, but she does not work in my field or department. I will not contact her since I doubt she can help me.

Remember when we discussed how many companies have incentive programs for employee referrals? I have never heard of such a program that places a restriction on referring candidates only within an employee's own department. You will also never know if a company has such a policy unless you ask your contact. If they do, they will happily refer your résumé. We have already documented the potential benefits of having "referred" status.

Even without such programs, an employee of a company or agency will also have some knowledge of the company's hiring policies and procedures. They can also pick up information regarding the department where the opening exists in terms of preferences, pending projects, atmosphere, and so on. Such information can allow a candidate to tailor his or her résumé and better prepare for an interview.

Tailoring your résumé for a particular job can involve deciding which projects to emphasize. You can also set yourself up as a better "fit" by indicating a few traits you have in common with the hiring manager. An employee could find that information out for you. If you are told, for instance, that the hiring manager firmly believes a résumé should not exceed one page, limit your résumé to one page.

Any similar information your contact can pass on could also help your interview preparation. When you know what projects and problems a company or department is working on, you know which of your talents or experience to start focusing on when you interview. Do not overlook intangibles—many hiring managers have "non-negotiable factors" or one vital question they ask all candidates. No matter what your qualifications are, you will never have a successful interview unless you satisfy the hiring manager on these issues. Here is a small sample of some immediate eliminators hiring managers have told me over the years:

- A sales manager told me that during the initial handshake he always glances at a candidate's shoes. If they are not perfectly shined, he will not hire the candidate, regardless of skills and interview performance. He believes that someone unwilling to take the time to shine their shoes and make themselves look their best will not always represent his company's products in the best light.

- An attorney charged with hiring new law school graduates for her firm believes that one vital quality lawyers need is the ability to think on their feet. At the initial interview, she spreads the candidate's submitted application paperwork (résumés, transcripts, letters, etc.) on the desk. She then asks the candidate to give her a reason to hire him or her she has not already read. The candidates who cannot answer this quickly are immediately eliminated.

- The owner of a landscape company asks every interviewed candidate the question, "Imagine if I were to pose you a question that, regardless what you answered, would change the course of your entire life. I then give you thirty minutes to come up with your answer. What steps would you take to make your decision?" He told me he wanted to see how someone went about making important decisions and how confident they are in making them. Do they say, "I'd call my mother/father/spouse"? This would indicate they had trouble making decisions. Over many years, the answers continue to amaze him.

- A human resource manager has her secretary hand every candidate the company's job application ten minutes prior to the interview and asks them to complete it. Any candidate who skips over the employment history section by writing "see résumé" and inserting a copy will not be hired. She views the application as the first potential assignment they are given. Skipping the section is viewed as omitting part of your first assignment on the job.

- No matter how well a candidate's interview goes, a program manager will not extend a job offer unless the candidate asks for the job. If the candidate is not excited enough about the position to request it, he or she will not have enough passion for the job to be successful.

As I stated, these stories represent just the tip of the iceberg. One should believe a good number of hiring managers have particular preferences. While I realize that some may not be totally fair, the bottom line is that *the decision maker believes that these are critical indicators of potential job performance.* Would you be grateful to know what factors are critical to a decision maker *prior* to an interview? Absolutely! Very often an existing employee, regardless of his or her department, can be a great source for such information.

I cannot close a discussion on preferences of a hiring manager without telling the following story. If you know any career navy people, ask them about job interview stories they have heard involving Admiral Hyman G. Rickover. He was famous for conducting "stress" interviews. The classic story several of them relate is his "meal test." According to this story, prior to extending any offer, the admiral would have a meal with the candidate. Rickover would closely watch the candidate once the first entree was served. If the candidate immediately salted or peppered the food without tasting it first, he would not extend him a job offer. He believed this was indicative of the candidate's unwillingness to test things, thus he would be prone to make assumptions. If I found out I had salted myself out of a job, I would never salt anything again in my life.

Self-Limiting Misconception Number Three: My friend/relative/ neighbor works in a different field than I do. I do not see how they could possibly help me in my job search. Why identify that I am looking for work and embarrass myself?

To understand why I discourage this thinking, try the following exercise:

    a. List all the jobs/careers/professions represented within your immediate family.
    b. Do the same for your closest circle of friends.

You probably come up with an amazing cross section of career fields. Have you ever referred a recently-graduated family member or friend to a member of this circle for job or career advice? Would you if asked? Most people I ask this indicate that they have or would. Why then do we assume that a friend/relative/neighbor would not do the same and open his or her network to us, even when this contact does not work in our field?

When you read reports on successful venues for job networking, notice that all of the groups are not necessarily field or profession specific. You will see names of groups, such as the chamber of commerce, small business associations, rotary clubs, alumni associations, five o'clock clubs, and so on. These groups have members representing countless fields and professions, and each member has a varied network of his or her own representing many fields. These members know and appreciate the value of a personal referral. They also have often given to and received from fellow members in fields other than their own countless referrals.

Our POAC program has held general networking meetings open to all participants as well as field-specific groups in varied professions over the years. Many customers often attend both meetings and report that they receive as many network leads from the general groups as from their field-specific meetings. One exercise we conduct in the general group has each participant introduce himself or herself to everyone. Each member indicates his or her profession and desired area of work. (This is great practice for one's "elevator speech.") During this exercise, contact leads often come from any member of the group, regardless of the profession—he or she just may know someone in the same field or at a company in that field.

A great example illustrating this point is the hiring story of Ann, a human resource director. Our staff knew that she had covered most bases in her job search. She served in an active capacity for both local and regional Society for Human Resource Management (SHRM) chapters. However, she reported that she found her job via a network lead completely unrelated to SHRM. Her son belonged to a tennis club's travel team. One day he played an extremely long doubles match, extending multiple hours. She spent most of the match talking with the mother of his partner. They had known each other as fellow club parents, but never really had talked much prior to this match. They each enjoyed the conversation, and when the match ended, the woman asked Ann what she did. Ann indicated she was an HR manager but currently between jobs. (Can you guess where this is going?) The woman worked for an investment company whose HR manager was scheduled to retire shortly. She instructed Ann to e-mail her a résumé so that she could forward it to the firm's VP. After two interviews, Ann was selected and hired. The job was never advertised.

Here are some final conclusions on this chapter:

If you are hoping for a short job search, starting the networking process will prove a more effective strategy toward that goal than delaying it.

Do not assume a contact from any area of your life has no means of helping you until you find this out for yourself.

Chapter 5

The Nervous Job Seeker

Self-Limiting Misconception Number Four: Embarrassment

While I do not wish to minimize or invalidate the feeling of loss one experiences with any type of unplanned job ending, what I do want any job seeker to understand is that *job loss and job failure are not synonymous.*

When unemployed individuals view job separation as a failure, embarrassment can easily dominate their psyche. Even with assurances from their previous employer that the cut was no reflection on their performance, many job seekers continually second-guess the reasons why *they* received the pink slip. I agree that a strong analysis of an entire situation surrounding a reduction in force is necessary for future career development. Study what happened; realize what warning signs were there and how to recognize them in the future. Think of ways to make yourself more "indispensable" to future employers. The biggest concern is when the feelings of failure hinder moving on with acquiring your next job.

Job seekers overwhelmed with shame about losing their previous job often dread making employment contacts. They immediately assume the recipient of any employment inquiry will want details about their "failure." They really fear being labeled a *loser* or *damaged goods.* This paralyzes many job seekers into the comfort of an anonymous job search, responding to ads and postings on the Internet, despite how limited the results of such a search probably will be.

If your main fear of networking revolves around the fear or

embarrassment described above, consider the following fact: *When making an employment contact, you do not have to reveal that you are out of work. Employed job seekers make networking contacts all the time; all the contact needs to know is that you are in the labor market.* Surprisingly, I have seen many job seekers become much more relaxed about making calls once they realize this.

Once candidates relax, they can focus more on describing their strengths, skills, abilities, and career goals. You need only address the reason for your search if asked—this is how any sales professional is trained to handle potential negatives about their product. You focus much more extensively on learning and communicating the *features* and *benefits* of the product and relating it to the needs of the employer. Remember the following sales mantra: *Never volunteer negative information.* Another noteworthy thing happens to the job seeker once he or she switches their focus to identifying their strengths as opposed to responding to their perceived weaknesses: *they gain more confidence.*

As a confidence builder, look over your résumé. For every job you've held, ask the following questions:

- What would my supervisor describe as my greatest strengths as an employee?
- What achievements in this job am I most proud of?
- What did my coworkers indicate they missed about me after I left?
- What testimonials did I receive?
- How did I make the operation better?
- What new skills did I acquire while employed there?

Write all your answers down. If you have saved previous evaluations or performance reviews, read them again. Realize how long and for how many different employers you made a positive difference. These methods parallel the way sales professionals study the features and benefits of their products. The more positives they remember, the more they can communicate them to a customer.

Now let's face another reality: *layoffs happen.* Prior to the 1990s, layoffs may have been more of a blue-collar phenomenon.

The recessions of the early 1990s and early 2000s hit many white-collar professional areas such as engineering, architecture, telecommunications, and information technology, to name a few. Even during strong times, job losses can result from mergers, acquisitions, company relocations, or outsourcing. The following chart is from the Bureau of Labor Statistics regarding incidents of mass layoffs and initial unemployment claims for the last ten years.

Number of mass layoff events and initial claimants for unemployment insurance, 1998-2007

Year	Layoff incidents	Number of initial claims
1998	15,904	1,771,069
1999	14,909	1,572,399
2000	15,738	1,835,592
2001	21,467	2,514,852
2002	20,277	2,245,051
2003	18,963	1,888,926
2004	15,980	1,607,158
2005	16,466	1,795,341
2006	13,998	1,484,391
2007	15,493	1,598,875
Avg.	16,877	1,821,057

Strong economic years are not immune to layoff incidents. All these statistics support a theory of mine: Over the past twenty years, if you have not experienced an unexpected job loss yourself, someone in your immediate circle of family or friends has. Most people I discuss this theory with agree. They all describe episodes where friends, family, and acquaintances faced job losses. Once someone describes such a scenario, I often ask if they perceived the person in question as a "loser." Most say not at all. So I ask next—why do people assume they will get the "loser" label when they face a job loss?

Believe it or not, one of the best tonics for alleviating the embarrassment factor is beginning to make network contacts, joining job clubs, or enrolling in job-search seminars. The job seeker then begins to realize how many other talented people have lost their jobs as well. Members attending our seminars report this as one of the things they appreciate most. After all participants introduce themselves, it becomes apparent that even professionals earning six-figure salaries are vulnerable to job loss.

Even while reaching out to individual contacts, you will often be surprised to realize many people you already know have experienced an unexpected job loss. There's an additional benefit to finding these individuals. Mark my word, anyone who has been in the job market recently will be happy to try to help in any way possible. He could well have learned the value of networking while seeking his current position. If it was a networking contact who introduced him to his current employer, he may feel that aiding a future job seeker allows him to indirectly repay the contact who provided him with the lead.

Borrowing from the film *Pay It Forward,* Steve Gallison encourages our graduates to provide job leads for existing customers. We provide an electronic job listing service to our customers. Job openings e-mailed to Steve for our specialized population are forwarded to the massive e-mail list we have generated over our many years of service along with application instructions. Leads sent by graduates carry a "Pay It Forward" tag in the subject line—this gives them the opportunity to give something back. Job seekers report a higher comfort level knowing the employer has hired a recently unemployed candidate with potentially similar characteristics and skills.

A career advisor or coach's greatest intrinsic reward comes when a customer returns to work. A huge incentive for me to write this book was the amazing collection of stories I have heard attesting to the power of networking in people's job acquisition process. Sharing such stories with the novice networkers I meet often has a greater impact on increasing their networking activity than throwing statistics at them. The next story illustrates the potential consequences embarrassment can have on job acquisition.

Joe was an electrical engineer who worked at a medium-sized engineering firm. (Stereotyping aside, most engineers are not great networkers, as they often have an introverted nature.) The company was scheduled to be acquired by a bigger engineering firm, with most of the employees due to benefit from the acquisition. As the deal came closer to fruition, however, the acquiring firm indicated it had no need for new electrical-based work. As a result, Joe and several other electrical engineers were let go. This was especially hard given that the majority of the firm's original staff was quite excited about the new employer.

The surprise loss of his job devastated Joe. The entire first month of his unemployment he remained in his house, only searching via newspapers and job boards. Not surprisingly, he received only a handful of calls and one interview, which failed to produce a follow-up. As the shock wore off a bit, Joe knew he had to alter his strategy. He began making a few networking calls in month number two, and started attending professional association meetings.

Joe described his neighborhood as "distantly friendly." It held an annual block party and people exchanged friendly waves and occasional small talk throughout the year. In Joe's seventh week of unemployment, as he was putting his trash out one evening, he spied his neighbor diagonally across the street doing the same. She greeted him with a friendly hello, and they exchanged a few pleasantries. She then mentioned that her children had seen him around during the daytime recently. She asked if he had been ill or had surgery.

As Joe told this story, he readily admitted that if this conversation had occurred in the first month of his job search, he would have easily latched onto the escape hatch she had offered about potential illness. Since his acceptance level had increased, Joe relayed that his company had been bought out and several staff had been laid off.

The neighbor expressed her condolences, indicating that layoffs were a sign of the times. Almost as an afterthought she asked Joe what he did. His reply, "I'm an electrical engineer," elicited a quick "You're kidding!" from the neighbor. She then informed Joe that she was the human resource manager for an engineering firm and that they had several openings for EEs since they had just been awarded some new projects. She asked for Joe's résumé, and her company eventually turned out to be Joe's next employer.

Reflecting back on his initial embarrassment, Joe still ponders "what might have been." Had the conversation occurred earlier in his job search and he failed to inform her of his situation, he may never have found the job. After he started with the company, he realized that all of the new jobs were filled with networked referrals and résumés on file.

Once again: Never assume a no on your own. Let the world tell you no.

Let's now address networking when you have experienced a termination or a similarly negative separation from your most recent position. If you were fired, just like a layoff, it happens. Columnist Joan Lloyd, on her Web site *Joan Lloyd at Work* (www.joanlloyd. com) references a recent survey indicating that sixty percent of CEOs report being fired at least once in their career. These individuals obviously rebounded.

As stated earlier, network calls do not require that you identify yourself as unemployed. There is also no need for you to identify yourself as "recently fired," either. Keep in mind that on your résumé, you never address the reason for leaving a job. The same applies for talking with networking contacts.

Sales professionals deal with negative publicity by focusing on a product's strong features and benefits. When a model receives negative publicity about a particular problem, do sales managers nationwide throw in the towel on their sales? No—they developed a strategy focusing more on its features and benefits; they addressed the negative information only when asked by a customer. Job seekers can to learn a lot from this strategy.

I want to close out this misconception with an observation. It should not surprise you that, given the populations I have worked with, I have come across many types of people ranging from tremendous "truth stretchers" to downright pathological liars. For many years, it amazed me how many of these people had little trouble finding employment. I finally realized one factor. They simply never address any past problems on their own. They might lie about them when asked, which I certainly do not advocate, but the bigger key to obtaining their jobs was *they did not worry about what they chose not to tell people.*

Having watched this behavior for years, you can imagine how

much it frustrates me to see honest, hard-working people focus their job search around the fear a potential employer may ask about their termination. In doing so, they fail to spend enough time inventorying and emphasizing many of their *strengths*. Sadly, they often lose job opportunities to less talented people who are not afraid to sing their own praises.

Self-Limiting Misconception Number Five: I have not spoken with this former colleague in X number of years. I feel very uncomfortable contacting him now that I am seeking employment—he might see my effort as transparent, only calling when I need something.

This is my "pet peeve" misconception! I see such a tremendous potential loss of resources for job seekers when they buy into this line of thinking. Professional peers in your field should make up the strongest members of your network—they work in your field of endeavor, know your talents, and have access to current professional information. They represent a potential pot of gold.

Let's face it—we all have forged some very satisfying interpersonal relationships at jobs. When a colleague changes jobs, we often feel the loss. It becomes more personal when we drift out of contact with the individual. We often say to ourselves, "I thought we were more than coworkers, but I guess he or she doesn't feel the same way." This disappointment is usually the reason why people are reluctant to reconnect.

Look at the reality of work-based relationships. An everyday coworker never requires planned contact—it occurs naturally through the requirements of each party's job. Once one colleague leaves, a new contact pattern needs to be established for regular contact to continue.

When a former colleague starts his new job, he quickly becomes overwhelmed by the adjustment. For the employee still with the previous company, the loss of the former colleague often puts added burden on his responsibilities. With both parties now facing a period of increased demands for their time, creating a new contact system becomes even more difficult to establish.

My point here is to show that when separated from a strong work relationship, we all intend to remain in contact with our professional friends. The natural circumstances surrounding a move, however, make keeping our pledge difficult. The majority of times, both parties share this responsibility for the contact lapse, and sincerely regret it.

When job seekers describe their reluctance to contact a former colleague for that reason, I love to ask, "Have you ever considered the possibility that he or she may enjoy hearing from you?" I often also add, "If you saw this individual in a public setting, would you hesitate to speak with him or her? What's the difference?"

Deep down, I believe we fear two possibilities. First, our contact might comment on the length of time since he or she last heard from us. Or, as previously stated, we worry about the perception that we only are calling because we need something.

If your ultimate fear focuses on the contact commenting on the time lapse since you last spoke, have a planned response. You can politely apologize, with a gentle reminder that communication lines work both ways. The opposite extreme would be a less polite response, as I once did in a situation I will share with you.

I had an acquaintance in my younger years I will call Sean. We hung out together with the same group of guys a few nights a week over a period of a couple of years. I then met and began dating the woman I would marry. Around the same time Sean took on a new job, so we drifted apart. One day we ran into each other at a local watering hole. While I greeted Sean warmly, indicating my gladness to see him, he responded quite coldly, basically asking what ill wind had blown me off the face of the earth.

Since his response annoyed me rather than activating any guilt pangs, I retorted, "I know, Sean, I'm real sorry, especially for not calling you after I heard about your accident."

"What accident?" he replied.

"The one that paralyzed your hands, disabling you from picking up a phone all these months yourself!"

While Sean may not have totally appreciated the sarcasm, I think he got the point. Lines of communication work both ways. In more than twenty years, I rarely have had to respond, politely or sarcastically, to comments about lapsed comments when greeting old friends. Much more often than not, the response is very positive. We have all been guilty of losing contact at some point. Do we hold this against everyone, or do we enjoy the chance to speak with an old friend or colleague? When an old colleague calls you out of the blue, what is your reaction—do you address the lack of contact, or are you glad to hear from him or her?

I understand a second possible fear here. If you previously had not found the time to contact an old colleague, how transparent does it look that only when you need something do you find time to contact him or her now? I cannot guarantee you that some old contacts won't have such a perception. What I *can* tell you is that most of the job seekers with whom I have discussed this report significantly more positive results from such contacts than negative. Once again, think about how you normally respond to any individual indicating to you that he or she has entered the job acquisition process, whether or not the choice has been voluntary or not. Most of us respond with more of a desire to help as opposed to analyzing the motives behind a call.

Former professional colleagues are vital contacts to job acquisition for another reason: the ever-changing nature of our economy. If you now face a job search, either by choice or involuntarily, I recommend trying the following exercise. Identify ten former coworkers from your last two to ten years with whom you have not spoken for some time. Contact all ten. First, see what percentage are happy to hear from you. Second, I will wager that at least two to three have been through some form of job search since your last contact. These individuals will embrace the chance to assist you once they hear you face the same situation. They know where you sit today—they sat in your seat some time ago and know the task you face. They also know what leads helped them. Such sources prove invaluable. If only one out of five provides good source information, that ratio comes out more favorably than the ratio of positive results from job boards or classified ads. And reconnecting gives you the opportunity to reminisce, which often refreshes your memory of projects and activities you performed and succeeded on. This proves valuable when preparing for future employer contacts, updating your résumé, or planning job interview strategies.

Finally, we all know how tough on our ego the job acquisition process is. The constant rejection, along with lingering self-doubts over the loss or dissatisfaction with our most recent job, can decrease our self-esteem. When this happens, displaying the energy level needed to effectively sell an employer on your skills becomes increasingly difficult. Chatting with a former colleague often lends itself to discussing successful projects on which you collaborated— this can go a long way toward recharging your self-esteem battery.

I will finish this misconception with another hypothetical situation. Imagine you are sitting in your first staff meeting on your next job. Your new company president announces a goal to develop a business relationship with Lisker Enterprises. As the president names of some of their key staff, one is Larry Barrenblitt. Your ears perk up since you worked with Larry for five years and became close friends. However, you last spoke with Larry about two and a half years ago. Do you:

> **A.** Inform the president that you and Mr. Barrenblitt are former coworkers and colleagues and volunteer to contact him immediately.

Or

> **B.** Think to yourself, "Wow, it's been a while since I've spoken with Larry and I'd feel odd calling him now to just try and get some business with him." You say nothing to the president.

Most of us, in this situation, would answer A. Unfortunately, an answer similar to B might be our choice when we're seeking a job on our own. What is wrong with this picture? You would overcome your anxiety about such a call to benefit your new boss, but you hesitate when you could be the prime beneficiary yourself?

So if embarrassment about needing a job or discomfort that you haven't spoken in a while holds you back from reaching out to an old colleague, take a leap of faith with me. Commit to making ten contacts outside of your comfort zone. Once you see how many of these people will be glad to hear from you, eager to help, and share similar job loss experiences of their own, you will be surprised you felt so nervous in the first place.

Chapter 6

The Naïve Job Seeker

Self-Limiting Misconception Number Six: I don't need or want anyone's help; I can find a job on my own.

Such is the mantra of what I term the Rugged Individualist Job Seeker (RI). The RI has always found jobs on his or her own. Even with personal or family connections to some high-ranking contacts with major companies, the RI refuses to contact them. He or she fears that "people will think I only got the job through who I know or what my name is." Even without established connections, RIs balk at accepting the "favor" of a lead from a colleague—he or she might expect some form of reciprocity and an RI never wants to feel obligated to anyone.

In our first self-limiting misconception, we discussed how daunting a task job acquisition can be. An RI candidate with the "do-it-myself'" syndrome faces the same hindrances to their search that the shy networker does. Without contacts, you are only accessing a small percentage of the potential job openings. I often wonder if the RIs realize that while they retain their pride, many jobs will be filled by candidates savvier to the realities of the labor market. Would you rather have your pride or a job?

When I discuss job search with an RI, I present the following questions. Think about all the speeches you have heard from successful people receiving awards. Remember books you have read where accomplished individuals describe their paths to success. How often do you hear the speaker or author say "I have no one to thank. I got where I am all by myself"? So far, no RI has cited such a case.

The Web site Themanager.org features a column from Chris Widener entitled "The DNA of Top Achievers." One "gene" Chris cited should be sobering to the RI mentality: the ability to see available resources and use them accordingly. "Those who are top achievers know that they cannot be Lone Rangers on the way to the top. No one makes it by himself or herself. Top achievers recognize their weaknesses—the weaknesses that if they don't cover will keep them from becoming a top achiever! They see their resources and work to get them into a helping position so they can continue the route to becoming a top achiever. And they don't use them, they utilize them. There is a big difference. People, finances, etc. are all brought in to help by the top achiever."

Let me share one seminar experience I had with an admitted RI named Mike, a finance manager. When the group discussed reasons for their lack of networking, he maintained that it was his desire to keep his job loss private and handle the search himself. He further described his recent embarrassment when one member of his softball team had attempted to contact him at his old job to be told Mike had been laid off. Much to his chagrin, this team member had informed the rest of the team about the job loss. At the next game, each teammate quietly approached Mike, expressed condolences and offered to assist in any way they could. One of the last players who talked with him revealed something Mike never knew. This teammate worked as a recruiter, specializing on positions in the financial field. The teammate gave Mike his card and requested he forward him a copy of his résumé ASAP.

I can tell you that what happened next makes every career search seminar facilitator's job very easy. Once Mike finished his story, the group reacted with a collection of positive responses—"Small world," "Great break," "I hope I find similar luck," etc. I then asked Mike about the feedback his recruiter teammate gave him on his résumé. He replied that he had not followed up with the recruiter since he still wanted to handle the search on his own. Talk about a group "turning" on a member. There were collective sighs and groans, and comments flew around the room, ranging from "Are you kidding?!" to "I'd *kill* for leads like that and *you turn them down!*" along with others that decency will not allow me to print in this space. Needless to say, that group reaction caused Mike to reevaluate his stance on flying solo.

The full range of job seekers I have worked with throughout my career, people at all income levels, often agree on one thing. Finding a job can, at times, be the toughest job or project they have ever tackled. To illustrate my point, do a little algebra. Factor the salary you desire as the "y" quotient in the following formula: (Y x 1.33) x Z. For the Z quotient, use how long you hope to hold the next job you seek.

I use this estimate to give the job seeker a sense of his or her value. The employer pays, in addition to salary, anywhere from twenty-five to forty percent of the salary in benefits, so splitting the difference, call it thirty-three percent. This gives a rough estimate of the value of the transaction you're discussing when applying for a job. (It's a conservative estimate, since we haven't even factored in overhead for office space, supplies, training, professional development, etc.) So if you seek a seventy-five thousand dollar per year job and hope to stay there five years, any job you apply for represents a transaction valued at over five hundred thousand dollars.

I also use this formula when presenting the following scenario to an RI. You receive a job offer. The company CEO informs you that your initial assignment will be to bring in an account, valued at a minimum of five hundred thousand dollars, in as short a time as possible. He then indicates that you will receive no contact lists, no leads, and no office support whatsoever. You must land this account totally through your own resources.

Would you accept this job offer? Well, that is essentially what you are doing when you choose to tackle a job search all by yourself.

Self-Limiting Misconception Number Seven: Networking is an imposition on busy people

One positive aspect to this misconception is that you will probably never develop into a "bad" networker. These people establish no rapport with contacts, focusing only on their own needs. They in no way hesitate to call an old colleague after a long period of no communication. The issue here is that they act as if they'd just spoken to them yesterday when they call. A fear of imposing grows out of a respect for people's time, which is a very positive quality. *Use this respect in your efforts to keep contacts as brief and concise as possible.*

I have three main points to make about the fear that networking imposes on someone's time.

Meeting a talented professional in any career track or profession is never an imposition on someone's time.

If you target your network calls appropriately, you should be speaking with key colleagues and decision makers in your field. How many of us think speaking with a fellow professional wastes our time? Over the years, we have received valuable insights from these conversations.

People enjoy discussing their careers or professions.

Read Dale Carnegie's *How to Win Friends and Influence People.* Carnegie stresses that you will always make a favorable impression on people when you focus the conversation of this person's interests. When you make a network call, you will speak with someone about his or her career or profession. This is clearly an area of *their* interest. This is something about which most people genuinely enjoy talking. Think about what you do when you want to start any conversation with someone you've just met—one of the first questions most people ask is about what the person does.

Sales professionals never view themselves as imposing on people's time.

Do not kid yourself by thinking the reason for this is either ego or that they are pushy—a key to their success is that they believe in their product. They know they have something to offer of value to a customer. *You* have talents and skills that can earn or save businesses money. You also have information about your profession that could benefit a fellow professional. Talking to you about this does not waste the time of someone committed to the success of her business.

I assure you that once you get some positive contacts under your belt, you will realize you have not imposed on anyone. As Nike says, "Just do it." This may seem simplistic, but it's the best way to start. *Pick up the phone and make some contacts.* How much time out of your life does an unsuccessful call take? Remember your goals. Once you start making quality calls to the right people, you will continuously discover the intrinsic values of these contacts.

Self-Limiting Misconception Number Eight: Government agencies have strict regulations covering their hiring process. Because the agencies must document adherence to these regulations, networking for government work will not be advantageous.

Any reader seeking work with the federal government may have come across the writings of Kathryn Kraemer Troutman, author of numerous books, including *Ten Steps to a Federal Job.* Her Web site is Résumé-place.com. Many people consider Kathryn as knowledgeable about the federal hiring process as anyone in the country.

The first of the ten steps Kathryn recommends in the book is *network.*[6] She documents several reasons why networking can play a prominent role in landing a job with the federal government. Many of these also apply to the hiring practices of state and local government agencies.

The best source to determine the federal job openings in your area is Usajobs.com. Check out this site and you will see that the volume of openings can be quite extensive. Sometimes a job will appear and the filing deadline may only be two to three days. Federal jobs require a detailed federal résumé, or OF-612. These documents take extensive time to prepare, especially when requiring written Knowledge Skills and Abilities (KSA) statements. Existing federal employees can provide a wealth of assistance throughout the entire process. They can also keep you informed about what openings will be coming up, allowing you time to prepare your paperwork for quick submission.

Federal vacancy announcements can be exceedingly difficult to understand. Ms. Troutman dedicates three full steps in her book to understanding the federal hiring process: review the federal job process (step two)[7], analyze core competencies for language (step four)[8], and analyze vacancy lists for keywords and government-type language (step five).[9] Employees who have worked for federal agencies can provide assistance in understanding each of these areas. They have earned their positions by understanding the process and allowing it to work for them, especially in the area of KSAs.

While state, municipal, and local government personnel processes may not be as complicated as the federal hiring process, they still have specific policies unique to each locale. Employees within the system can provide you with information to increase the viability of your application. If the employee is not especially well-versed in his or her agency's hiring methods, he or she can easily direct you to a colleague who is. I have worked in state government for thirteen years. You quickly learn, in any department you go to, which employees have the best understanding of "the process" in getting hired or promoted.

Keep another reality in mind about government work: No matter how many personnel rules and policies are written to ensure all applications receive "fair and equal" consideration, smart hiring managers know how to work their candidates through the system. If a high ranking official needs a job "favor" for a friend, there are ways to get the process moved in the right direction. One highly-experienced program manager I know and respect regularly tells his staff, "If you desire a position within a government agency and have an elected official as a personal contact, do not hesitate to use him or her. If not, you may lose out on a job to a less-talented candidate unafraid to call their elected contact to help out his or her candidacy."

To conclude the discussion of government jobs, I will share with you a great account of how networking played a huge role in a customer landing a job with the United States Government Printing Office (GPO). An accountant customer of our program had followed a layoff by working steadily through placement firms, including a one-year contract with a non-profit organization. While he earned good money in these capacities, he wanted something more permanent. Bill enrolled in our three-day seminar and began to accept the reality that he needed to expand his networking.

He decided on an action plan. As an alumnus of a large, Catholic boys' high school in the Baltimore area, he prepared a letter outlining his full career experiences and skills. Using the alumni directory, he sent a copy to all graduates listed within six years of his graduation year. During this process, he discovered that a classmate of his was comptroller of the GPO. The comptroller kept his résumé and advised him of when appropriate openings would be forthcoming. Once a particular accountant opening became available, he instructed his classmate to submit his federal résumé. After completing the full selection process, our customer was hired. While it took nearly eight months from Bill's initial résumé contact until his start date, it proved to be worthwhile. His classmate also served as his agency mentor and has helped guide him to a promotion.

That concludes what I have observed to be the core self-limiting beliefs about the networking process encountered over my years in the career services profession. Countless job seekers I have met rate their own networking at a "C" grade or below, yet know little about how to improve it. After some discussion, they often realize that one or more of the listed misconceptions serves as the main barrier towards increasing their network activity. Once they understand how false or limiting the conceptions are, they then report steady improvement in their networking. Hopefully, readers will recognize some of these misconceptions as the reasons why they do not network as much as they need to. Once a perception is identified as a misconception, eliminating it from one's belief system becomes easier. When that barrier lifts, increased networking can begin.

I will next outline a list of daily reminders designed for trying to upgrade your networking, then address specific strategies of the networking process.

Chapter 7

Twelve Daily Tasks to Improve Your Job Networking

Committing to improving a weakness in your life requires daily attention. A former supervisor of mine preached, "Do something new for a minimum of twenty-one consecutive days and it becomes a habit." That philosophy has always worked well for me. The following is a list of guidelines you should review on a daily basis. Adhering to them should greatly enhance your networking ability. I will also provide additional strategic guidelines in the following chapters.

As in any other area of life, once you identify a weakness, practice will be needed to improve it. In a recent golf lesson, when my instructor asked about the weakest part of my game, I admitted to the short game; chipping and putting. When he next asked how often I work on this at a practice range or before a round, I realized I rarely do. I once again repeated to myself "Definition of insanity: Doing the same thing over and over again and expecting different results."

1. **Make a minimum of two contacts per day (or a predetermined time period) that are beyond your normal comfort range.**
   You need to establish a commitment to making the type of calls you have avoided in the past. Once you compile a contact list, scroll down the list and rate each contact on the level of comfort you feel in making the contact. Start calling the contacts you have a minimal discomfort level with. Then move through the list in that order.

Tips

- At the very beginning, make calls to the contacts that have LESS potential or you are not as interested in. Give yourself a chance to practice your delivery and make adjustments. This way, you will be less likely to make mistakes with the more important contacts you wish to make. This strategy works well when attending a job or career fair.

- Select the time of day when your energy level is greatest. This will vary from person to person. (If you are a true "night owl" this could be a problem, as some people may not appreciate being called at midnight or later.)

- Each new week, go back to the master list and rank your contact list again. As time goes along, you should be able to look back and see that calls that once seemed out of your comfort range now present little to no anxiety.

2. Never assume a no.

We examined at length how job seekers often talk themselves out of a network contact. You never know if a person might have a lead or information unless you ask. Many of the successful networking examples cited throughout this book would never have come to fruition had the job seeker initially viewed the contact person as an assumed no.

I realize that in no other venture of life do we hear the word no or face more repeated rejection than we do during the job acquisition process. Not to diminish the toll this takes a job seeker over the course of job acquisition time, but is rejecting yourself the answer? This is essentially what assuming a no does.

3. Target the "decision maker."

A key to successful marketing and sales lies in determining what individual at a company will decide whether the product or service is purchased or not. Many job seekers contact a company's human resource office. That department often only finds out about potential openings once they are ready for posting. Other job seekers immediately call the company president or CEO. He or she might refer you to the right individual, but chances are before you reach them, you will face extensive screening by an assistant or secretary.

Once you identify a company that has the potential need for someone with your skills and talent, determine the individual within the company you most likely would report to. Ultimately, that person would likely have the final say in your hiring. This is the person you want to market yourself to.

For assistance in this area, you may want to speak with business-to-business sales professionals or read some sales training materials. Finding the decision maker is vital to their jobs. They can offer many tips on studying a company to determine your target contact. A wealth of suggestions can be found in sales training books and materials.

4. Perfect your introduction (thirty-second commercial or elevator speech).

Catching the attention of a contact as quickly as possible is vital. You must develop a means by which to introduce yourself that immediately tells the contact who you are and what you offer. I discuss this speech in greater detail in the next chapter. It requires daily practice and refinement.

5. Focus all contacts on seeking advice rather than specific job openings.

This places the contact in the expert status and opens the door to his or her network of contacts as well as knowledge of the field or company. Introduce yourself as an individual seeking career information. Describe your talents and areas of expertise (elevator speech), then ask the contact for feedback or recommendations on places you can look. If you make a positive impression on the contact, he will reveal any opportunities at his company. This reinforces the importance of rule number three. You are much more likely to receive helpful advice or information from a professional within your field of specialty than from one in another department.

Tip
An excellent way to assure a contact that you are seeking advice rather than potential job openings is to schedule information interviews. Ask the contact to meet for fifteen to twenty minutes for coffee. Similar to cold calls, while seeming scary at first, once you try it a few times, you will be surprised how much easier this becomes.

6.   Offer the contact something beneficial.

Networking is a relationship-building process and works best when both parties benefit. You probably have information and contacts that could benefit a fellow professional even more than they can help you. Offer your own network or expertise as part of the relationship.

7.   Show appreciation to people who offer helpful advice.

This may seem like common sense, but it does not happen often enough. If you re-contact someone to thank him or her for a lead he or she gave you, he or she not only is grateful, but develop a very positive initial impression of you. We know what the old cliché says about opportunities for a first impression. Thanking the person in writing provides an added bonus. It gives you the opportunity to describe yourself more and enclose a résumé.

8.   Always ask for additional contact names.

In any contact you make, finish up by asking if he or she knows of anyone else you might call for leads or information. If you have made a good impression on a fellow professional but he or she has no immediate needs at their company, they will happily refer you to a colleague. This helps their relationships among their fellow professionals. Ask if you can mention that he or she referred you. Often this can establish credibility, making reaching that contact easier.

9. The more people that know you are seeking a job, the more potential leads you will get. Be open to any situation as having potential.

As addressed in rule number two, you will never find out how extensive an individual's own network is unless you ask. Keep all pipelines plugging. Once the process gets rolling, you will be amazed at the variety of sources from which you receive helpful contacts.

Here is an example from a client. As part of Alex's search, he hoped to develop an inside contact at the Securities Exchange Commission (SEC). He had been working on this for a while with no luck. One weekend, he and his wife volunteered to provide a chaperone for their daughter's Girl Scout ski trip. His wife announced that it would be easier for him to chaperone the trip, since she was employed and he was not. (Spouses will occasionally play that trump card on you during periods of unemployment.) There were twenty-three other chaperones on the trip; twenty-two were mothers. But this cloud had a silver lining. Guess where the only other father on the trip worked? The SEC! Alex now had a contact.

10. Establish a network e-mail list.

Put together a list of all the people who have indicated a desire to assist you in job acquisition. E-mail the group on a regular basis to update them on your status.

This serves many great purposes. It will limit the number of follow-up calls you need to make. Contacts with no new information might avoid these calls. The list allows responses from those with helpful information. Also, it keeps your name on the minds of your network list. Typically, when you first approach someone, he or she suggest people he or she may know who can help immediately. However, he or she can easily get busy and lose sight of your needs. With regular reminders, one day something may roll across his or her desk that's in your interest. E-mail also enables him or her to contact you easily. Include items of interest (good articles, etc.) so that the recipients get used to enjoying your e-mails. Be careful when using humor, because not everyone shares the same sense of humor.

At the end of the book, I'll show you a great thank-you letter a job seeker sent his network once he received a job.

11. Remember that improving your network is a marathon, not a sprint.

You will not become a "Grade A" networker overnight. Have patience and give yourself a break when things move slowly. Evaluate your progress in terms of both increased comfort levels, as well as results.

12. Once you get your next job, continue to build your network.

Learn from how hard you needed to work to build your network list up. Continuously reach out to others in both personal and professional settings. As an added bonus, you may have the chance to network someone else into a job lead or new position. The level of personal satisfaction is tremendous.

Chapter 8

Getting the Process Going

Networking your way to a new job will challenge and enhance your organizational skills. Start the process with an action plan.

Tip

To assist in tracking your job search contacts, consider using the Web site JibberJobber.com. It provides a free basic service to track places you have contacted and applied.

Here are some steps you need to take:

Step 1. Develop your contact lists.

Break your contact lists into three categories: professional, potential employers, then family, friends, and acquaintances. Start with professional. Look at your résumé. On a separate sheet of paper, for each of your previous jobs, write down the names of people at each job whom you enjoyed working. Also include anyone who you know appreciated your talent. This includes clients, customers, vendors, and so on. Rank them in order of your comfort level in contacting them. Do this for every job, school, training class, or professional association on your résumé.

On this and subsequent lists, put telephone numbers next to names if you have them. When you do not have phone numbers, try Internet phone directories or running the names through Google or another search engine. See if you can locate them on LinkedIn, Facebook, or other social networking sites. In addition to phone numbers, you may find people's new jobs or employers. If you have no luck locating contact information on your own, keep in mind that some of the other contacts you make may be able to let you know how to reach them.

Tip

If you discover a colleague has moved to a new position or company, this can serve as an opening line for your contact. Start the call by indicating you have just discovered his or her new position.

The next list you develop will be of potential employers. Find as may companies, businesses, or agencies within your commuting distance that may need someone with your skills and talent. Libraries have local directories of businesses under designated categories. Another great source for these can be local Economic Development Offices. They not only have detailed lists of businesses in the area, but they know what businesses plan to locate there in the near future.

Tip

Ask if you can speak with someone at the Economic Development Office and provide him or her with a résumé. One of the primary functions of Economic Development Offices is assisting new businesses moving into the area. They welcome the opportunity to refer talented candidates to a new employer.

Plan to do some more research once you get company lists. As I state in the twelve daily rules, you need to identify the right contact within the company. What individual will have the final say in your hiring? This is not as complicated as you might think. Often the main telephone contact can tell you this if you ask the right question. Say you are a purchasing specialist. Call and ask for the name of the purchasing manager. Other ways can involve rolling through the Web site of the company. I have known job seekers to go to a company's Web site and after the URL put "/directory" or "/chart" and sometimes get listings of the phone directories or organizational charts that lists the names. More detailed business directories may have this.

Tip

Many directories list the number of employees the business has. Pay special attention to the small and medium-size businesses. Studies show that nearly two-thirds of all new jobs are created by small businesses. As documented earlier, these companies struggle with posting or advertising any openings due to costs and staff time involved in reviewing numerous résumés. Such an operation would welcome contact from a potentially qualified candidate.

Your third list will be of family, friends, and acquaintances. Ask yourself the following question: How many people know I'm looking for work? The more people who know, the more individual networks will become open to you. Do not only include people on this list with higher level jobs. Put down anyone who might be willing to assist you. Rank these also in terms of your comfort level contacting them.

A second method for brainstorming contact lists I received from a recruiter friend, Lisa Wiley Parker, principal of Competitive Matrix, LLC. Lisa has identified and prioritized potential network sources for seminars she conducts on networking. She recommends looking first for people you know who are heavily involved in hiring or business services, such as:

→ Outplacement counselors

→ Human resource professionals

→ General or specialized recruiters

→ Staffing agency personnel

→ Industry association officers

→ Chamber of commerce members

→ Economic development office professionals

→ Reporters for business journals

Next you should think of your contacts whose professions or stature naturally provides them with a large number of contacts:

→ Commercial and personal accountants

→ Commercial and community bankers

→ Attorneys

→ Politicians

→ Alumni association officers

→ Business owners

Third, think of anyone you know working in a profession that serves businesses. He or she can provide a wealth of potential contacts. A list of possibilities includes:

→ Commercial realtors

→ Corporate insurance agents

→ Consultants

→ Telephone systems sales representatives

→ Office furniture sales representatives

→ Software sales representatives

→ Outsourced payroll professionals

→ Couriers and office supply delivery personnel

Last, put together a list of people providing services to you. They provide services to people from many walks of life and could be a link you need. Consider your:

→ Financial planner

→ Health care providers

→ Cosmetologist

→ Athletic trainer

One final recommendation Lisa makes is to include anyone you know who recently found work. He or she may still have active opportunities and can let you know what has and hasn't worked for him or her.

Many of you will look at this list and never feel comfortable discussing your career situation with people in many of these categories. Please remember, this list is designed to help generate ideas. Even if eighty percent of the suggestions are not people you would feel comfortable contacting, the list could make you consider someone who you otherwise might not have considered as a potential source.

You will discover that most of your contacts will express a desire to help you but may not know how to. Make it easier for them. First, they must know what your skills and talents are, along with what setting would best utilize those skills and talents. A résumé may not always reflect this clearly. Develop a written summary of your goals to include it as an introduction to your résumé. Send the contact these documents. Indicate that you will e-mail him or her regularly with updates on your status, as part of your e-mail network list mentioned in the twelve daily rules chapter.

A network e-mail list serves many great purposes. You can easily remain in contact and on the minds of your contacts without spending much time on the telephone. With these regular reminders, people are more likely to remember your needs when they hear of something potentially beneficial for you. The e-mail allows them to respond if they have any information, and ignore if not. Most will prefer this to handling a follow-up phone call if they have no news for you.

Step 2. Start using an online networking site.

Numerous sites on the Internet allow you to research contacts and companies, find common contacts, and obtain information. These sites include Facebook, LinkedIn, Plaxo, and many others. Once you join, you set up your profile outlining your talents, your work history, and your specialties. You then invite people to join your list of connections; people who you trust and who respect your professional capabilities. Having someone in your network allows you to view their connections. Members can also join groups based on common interests like professions, alumni, or geography.

Colleagues can then introduce you to members within their connections list. You can also look up select companies and see if you have any connections to anyone working there and request an introduction.

LinkedIn has quickly cornered the market in recent years as the prime online business networking site. As of July 2009, it has more than forty-three million users, up from thirty million at the end of 2008. An excellent book available to help with this site is *I'm on LinkedIn—Now What? A Guide to Getting the Most Out of LinkedIn* by Jason Alba. He also has a very helpful blog at Imonlinkedinnowwhat. com. Another helpful site is Linkedintelligence.com.

Keep in mind a point Alba constantly stresses in his writing. LinkedIn makes finding connections much easier. What it does not do is take the place of you making contact once a connection is established.

Step 3. Join a job club.

Find a group of people in your area also searching for work. Ideally, the group will specialize in your profession. However, clubs serving job seekers from all fields of work can also be just as effective. Job-Hunt.org and *The Wall Street Journal's* Careerjournal. com, to name a couple, offer lists of groups within each state. Local employment service offices may either hold job clubs or maintain lists of ones within their area. Word of mouth can also provide leads as well as listings in the community events section of local newspapers.

The first benefit of such a group can come from just seeing the types and number of people searching work. Realizing that many other talented people are between jobs, either in your field or other fields, often relieves many of the feelings of failure that can accompany a job loss.

If the group is specific to a career track, you can receive up-to-date information on that labor market in your area. Members who come across opportunities that do not fit their needs can pass the leads on to other members. Interview trends, buzzwords, Web resources all can be discussed. Job clubs also provide opportunities to do interview role-plays and share negotiation tips. Fellow professionals often provide the most objective feedback about the realities of the market.

Family members may misapply pressure to either extreme in their support of a job seeker. Due to the financial hardships unemployment brings, justly stressed family members often seek a quick resolution. The job seeker feels this while evaluating potential job opportunities. An objective fellow professional can better evaluate a job for potential flaws. This could prevent you from accepting what may prove to be a dead-end job, or worse, a position that could land you back to unemployed status a short time down the road.

At the opposite end of the spectrum, some job seekers can be overly selective, especially in the early stages of their job search. Family members can also support this, out of pride, not wanting a diminished standard of living. Job club members who have experienced the current labor market for lengthier periods of time can point out that an offer, while not as strong as the situation you left, could be about as strong as what other members have seen for a while. Sadly, in the many years I have spent dealing with people who were out of work, I often see candidates turn down offers early in their search. Then they find the lapse in employment lasts several months and unemployment benefits lapse. The offers they turned down suddenly look mighty good. Worse, they end up accepting an inferior offer.

Tip

One thing I stress to any candidate contemplating a job offer: trust your instincts. If some issue about the offer, company, or supervision makes you feel hesitant, there probably is a reason for this. Most of us can look back to job decisions we lived to regret and remember some warning signs we ignored prior to accepting the job. The above-mentioned family pressures can often blind these instincts.

One other plug for job club participation. If you are contemplating turning a current job loss into a chance to switch careers, new contacts can provide more objective feedback about this than old friends, family members, or colleagues. These people have always known you in your previous field. The thought of you switching careers can be scary to them, as many people fear change. New contacts do not view you in your previous role, and have no such trepidation.

Tip

When becoming involved in a group or as part of your job search in general, gravitate toward people with positive attitudes. Another friend and colleague of mine, Nancy Fink, regularly warns job seekers to stay away from toxic people. They can be easy to find among the ranks of the unemployed.

Step 4. Perfect your "introduction commercial."

A key to successful networking lies in how quickly and concisely you can introduce yourself to someone and demonstrate what you have to offer. This is often called your introduction commercial or elevator speech. The speech must contain essential elements of your message. *The Sales Bible: The Ultimate Sales Resource* by Jeffrey Gitomer and *Elevating Your Elevator Speech: A Powerful Way to Answer the Question "What Do You Do?"* by Dave Sherman have great resources for developing your speech. These books primarily focus on tools sales professionals use when introducing themselves during interactions like cold phone calls or trade shows.

The job seeker must modify these techniques for the job search mode. Katherine Hansen does a great job of breaking down the changes for Quintessential Careers Web site (www.quintcareers. com). She parallels the elements of a tailored sales speech to job seekers.

Sales Professional	Job Seeker
Who I am.	Same.
What business I am in.	What field or industry I am in.
What customers I serve.	What position or capacity I serve.
How I differ from my competition.	What are my unique skills and abilities.

What benefits do customers derive from my product or service.	What benefits can employers derive from my skills, based on previous accomplishments.

To perfect the speech use the process of Script, Practice, and Rehearse (SPR). Once you develop your speech, constant practicing and rehearsing will continually improve it. When you think about it, SPR is nothing new. When we face a potentially important or unpleasant interaction, we SPR what we plan to say, don't we? The more we give our introduction, the more confident we will feel about presenting it each time. Try to keep a thirty-second time limit on the speech. Practice in front of a mirror. Better yet, videotape yourself and review it. This process greatly enhances any type of speech.

I frequently ask anyone who makes public performances (singers, actors, etc.) about the anxiety they experience before a performance. They often report that any nervousness usually occurs prior to stepping on stage, then dissipates once they begin performing. The primary reason for this is that once they begin performing, they are doing something they have rehearsed countless times. I remember hearing a comment from John Paxson of the Chicago Bulls, after hitting a shot that clinched the NBA Championship. When asked if he was nervous during the shot, Paxson simply replied "No! Do you know how often I have practiced that shot throughout my basketball career?"

Most introverts realize the need for a script or outline. Unfortunately, many extroverts need one also, but fail to recognize this. Because they have little to no fear of talking with strangers, they believe the speech will take care of itself. This can lead to rambling and excessive verbiage, which wastes the time of the prospect and causes a loss of interest. The faster you touch on a topic that interests the listener, the closer attention the listener will pay to you. Always remain sensitive to a person's time.

Researching the contact can greatly enhance the chances of getting him or her interested. Prior to contacting an individual, try to find out what projects she is working on or planning for. What issues does she face currently? If you then begin the contact by referencing a skill or experience you have that can address one of her main issues, you stand a much better chance of gaining her attention. Often the source that refers you to the individual can provide some insight to her needs. If not, research the person or company similar to the way you would research preparing for an interview.

Step 5. Start making contacts.

Before making any calls, first rank your potential contacts by level of familiarity.

Level I

Level I contacts are cold calls to places where you have no prior contact. Obviously, this is the least favorite contact of even seasoned sales professionals. A common perk offered to experienced sales reps is the elimination of most cold calls. They have sales trainees, or support or telemarketing staff qualify leads for them.

Since even many experienced sales professionals disdain and avoid cold calls, novice networkers tend to avoid them also. Unfortunately, they do not have that luxury. A thorough job search should include identifying and reaching out to companies or agencies you desire to work for. Without an inside referral, most candidates submit a résumé either via mail or online. However, one can increase the chances of his or her résumé receiving a favorable review with an established internal contact. At times, a cold call might be the only way to establish such a contact. Target the individual who would likely be your supervisor within the company. The more individuals you reach with the ability to hire you, the greater your chances of becoming a serious candidate.

Interestingly, some job seekers prefer cold calling over calls where they have some familiarity. With no previous familiarity, they figure "What's the damage if the call doesn't work out?" Jeffrey Gitomer stresses a similar theme in *The Sales Bible: The Ultimate Sales Resource*. He recommends treating cold calls as great rehearsals for more vital contacts. Start out with potential employers you have little to no interest in. Monitor how you progress in generating interest.

See how your comfort level improves. As futile as it may seem, your rate of generating interest will still most likely exceed that of mailing résumés and posting your résumé online. If you know you need work in this area and struggle, read the chapter on cold calling in *Knock Your Socks Off Selling* by Gitomer and Ron Zempke. They recommend a variety of techniques to help with tackling cold calls.

Level II

With Level II calls, you have some familiarity with the contact. Either you have been referred by a colleague or have met the contact previously. You need to immediately establish your familiarity by either indicating your referral source or where your previous contact was. Some feel that a follow-up to a submitted résumé is at this level while others believe that following up after a résumé is a cold call. Decide for yourself what level such a call is.

Level III

With Level III contacts you have some sort of relationship, such as former colleagues, family, or friends. The recipient will recognize your name but may need to be informed of the reason for the call.

I break these levels out so you can label each call you plan to make on a given day. Try to schedule a good mix of each level.

Tip

Avoid the temptation to use all your Level III calls first. You may need one as a morale booster later on in your call sequence.

Set and stick with goals as to how many calls per day you will make. Select a time of the day when your energy level is high. A morning person should try to make their calls before the lunch hour. I had success focusing the calls between 10:00 and 11:30 AM to avoid both the busy start of the day and lunchtime. If you communicate better later in the day, afternoon calls could work better for you. Once again, to avoid post-lunch and late-day rushes, make calls during 1:30 and 4 PM. Both of these strategies may need to change if it is difficult to reach your desired individual. We will discuss this more later on.

One of the first hurdles you may face occurs when targeting a particular employer or company. If you have no contact name, do not make the mistake of calling the main number and inquiring about potential job openings. The person who answers likely will refer you to either the Web site, human resources, or inform you they are not hiring. The best way to get a contact name is to first browse the company Web site, or type the company name along with your department into a search engine to see if you come up with a name. Should these efforts fail, try one or more of the following steps:

- Call the main number and ask for the name of the individual in charge of the department you are interested in. (Yes, sometimes it is that simple.) You can then either ask to be connected with him or her or call at a later time. Advantages to the later call will be addressed shortly.
- You may be asked the purpose of the call. If so, be direct in a manner that will decrease your chances of being referred to human resources or elsewhere. State "I am a (your profession) and wish to discuss his/her department operations." Be as polite and confident as possible. Indicating that you are inquiring about job openings may prevent you from reaching the department head. Switchboards often have a policy regarding where to refer employment inquiry calls. If this does not generate a name, many people have found the name of department heads by saying they need to correspond with such-and-such department head. If you use this method, do not identify yourself.
- Check to see if the main answering system allows you direct access to certain departments. Often, once within the department, the voicemail system will give you a menu.

Once you have a name, try to access a dial-by-name system,

if available. Also, remember if you ever receive a direct extension number, use it. Your chances of reaching an individual increase without an intermediary involved.

Tip

Another method for reaching decision makers can be calling before or after normal business hours. The call screeners may not yet be in or have left for the day, but a manager-level individual may still be there. I used to find that a great day on which to reach many decision makers was a bad weather day. Many support staff opt out, but the higher-level individuals make it in, and often are the ones answering the phones.

When dealing with call screeners, be as polite and professional as possible. This will increase your chances of being referred to your desired destination. Being overly aggressive or deceitful can potentially backfire. Sales professionals are trained in a variety of methods to get past call screeners. Some can be quite unsavory. Keep in mind that a sales representative will have minimal contact with other staff in his or her pursuit of a sale. As a job seeker, you need to realize that you could possibly work at this establishment one day. I once learned a valuable lesson at a training session on sales. While discussing methods to get past call screeners, an attendee mentioned that she worked for several years as an office manager. She views call screeners as an ally, not an adversary. Based on her experience, she knew what type of caller she was most likely to forward. In addition, the call screener can provide valuable information to a potential job seeker if approached respectfully and politely.

When you start to make calls, have your introductory commercial outlined in front of you with points you want to be certain you make. Here are the possible scenarios you may face. Be prepared for each, as the more professional and relaxed you sound, the better your chances of making a positive impression.

- **Direct line to your desired target.** If the call is answered, proceed directly into your introduction commercial.

If you get a voicemail, proceed with your "voicemail policy," which I will address later. Many times after a designated number of rings, a direct call may "roll over" to an attendant. Usually this process is recognizable with a shorter sequence between rings. Many people hang up before an attendant picks up to avoid leaving a message if they want to use the direct number.

- **You know your contact's name and the call is answered by another party**. Politely request to speak with the individual by name. If asked the reason for the call, state that you want information regarding his or her department's operation. If someone has referred you to the individual, identify your referral and that he or she suggested you call. The person may again ask for the reason of the call. Stay with the request for information. You may be told the party is unavailable. If offered his or her voicemail, go to "voicemail policy."

- **You contact a company without knowing your desired contact's name**. First, request to speak with the manager or director of the department or area you are interested in. You may be forwarded immediately. If you are asked the reason for the call, follow the same steps mentioned above. Sometimes you may be told the party is unavailable. Ask when the best time to call is and get the name. If offered the party's voicemail, take it regardless of whether you leave a message or not. Most of the time, you'll be able to get his or her name or direct number from the voicemail. Then you can ask directly for him or her on your next call. If there is no voicemail, consider leaving a message or just indicating you will call back.

- **What to do about voicemail**? Handle this however you feel most comfortable. If you have received feedback that you have a strong, concise introductory speech, then leave that on the voicemail. An impressive message increases the likelihood of a callback. If you have a referral name, include that with your message.

Tip

Whenever you attempt a strategy for the very first time, practice the process on employers or contacts you have only mild interest in. That way, any errors or gaffes will have limited damage. Once you have perfected your delivery, move on to more critical contacts.

Finally, be prepared to arrange a follow-up process. Remember when closing out any discussions, ask these questions:

- Find out if he or she has any interest in reviewing your résumé.

- Ask if he or she can recommend anyone else you might benefit from contacting.

- Establish a time frame for your next contact. If the party is noncommittal on a response, suggest a time yourself.

- Be vigilant about following up. By seeing how conscientious you are about checking back, the contact will realize that you will be as conscientious an employee.

Many job seekers find comfort in sending a blind résumé and making their initial contact the follow-up to see if the résumé has been received. The problem they face is pinning their opening solely on the question, "Did you receive or review the résumé I sent?" What happens if he or she has not reviewed it? Many unsolicited résumés are immediately sent to human resources. Mailing first does not diminish or eliminate the need to develop a strong opening introduction.

Step 6. The contact.

Tip

Whenever you make a career-related call, conduct the call standing up and near a mirror. Your voice sounds stronger while on your feet, as verified by countless customers from broadcast-related fields. Use the mirror to ensure that you smile frequently. Trainers for telephone sales and customer service personnel maintain that call recipients notice the difference when a caller smiles.

Once you reach your desired contact, quickly introduce yourself and proceed with your "commercial" When you rehearse this, try to stick to a thirty-second time range. This will keep you from rambling excessively. Once you have completed your introduction, wait for a response. Sometimes, when a period of silence occurs, the discomfort causes the caller to begin speaking more. This is often ad-libbed and can easily come across as rambling or unfocused. Develop the patience to wait for a response.

If the response seems positive, begin probing him or her about his or her immediate needs and the contact's assessment of the current business market. As we have mentioned several times before, focus the contacts more on seeking general advice. You will receive much more beneficial information. Do not hesitate to share knowledge you have obtained throughout your own research. Networking is a mutually beneficial process.

The ideal goal is to try to schedule an informal meeting, often referred to as an "information interview." An easy option is a coffee meeting. It poses limited infringement on someone's schedule. When you ask, you will be surprised how much more often you will receive a meeting than you anticipated. One of the first lessons I learned about trying to schedule meetings was to offer two time periods rather than an open ended "Could we meet?" This forces the person to pick the better of available times.

Should this not be possible, suggest a résumé exchange and set up a time frame for a follow-up. Ask if e-mail is a potential method of following up. Always make absolutely certain you show appreciation for the contact's time and information. If he or she gives you his or her e-mail address, drop them a quick thank you. You can also mail him or her a thank-you note.

During the contact, make sure you have the ability to take notes. Use a personal digital assistant, day planner, or program such as JibberJobber to record follow-ups.

Keep at it! You're bound to have some mishaps, so do not become too self-critical. Look back at each contact and critique yourself in a manner that will improve your subsequent contacts. Be prepared. You will get blown off or have people treat you rudely at times in the process. Try your best not to take this personally.

Step 7. Follow up!

If one of your contacts is interested in your skills, the next critical judgment of you occurs with the precision of your follow-up.

Tip

When sending a follow-up résumé, make sure you make adjustments for the reader's interests. Hopefully you gained some insight into the contact's interests during your conversation. Show your appreciation for their time in the cover letter, along with additional information selling your skills.

Next, list the scheduled time to reach out to your contact again in your master schedule. Jot down notes about your conversation to have available at your next call. If you are extremely resourceful and efficient about your job search, you will be perceived as equally skilled as an employee.

Conducting a thorough job search will definitely challenge your organizational skills, but the end results will prove worth the effort.

One final factor regarding follow-up. Remember how we stress that networking is about long-term relationship building. Once you accept a job offer, contact the people who have provided any level of assistance. Let them know of your opportunity and thank them once again for their assistance. If you believe you may have a chance to do business with them in your new role, doing this goes a long way in helping you maintain your network should you need it in the future.

This chapter covered a lot of material, so here are the key points:

- Start with an action plan.
- Develop lists of contacts.
- Use an online networking site such as LinkedIn.
- Join a job club.
- Continuously work on refining your introduction speech.
- Commit to making the time and effort for contacts.
- Stick with a script or outline.
- Make sure to follow up.

Chapter 9

Networking Events

So far we have focused mostly on telephone contacts. Now let's look at the big, bad world of in-person networking events. Here you lose the anonymity the telephone provides. While this strikes fear into the heart of many a novice networker, keep in mind what any sales professional will tell you. Given the chance, he or she would much rather deal face-to-face than via the telephone with a potential customer. In-person meetings provide the opportunity to make a much more favorable impression. This can create a distinct advantage over candidates they only see on paper.

Networking events can include professional association meetings, chamber of commerce mixers or events, or trade shows—the list goes on and on. Any event designed to gather a group of either general or specialized business people together can be a networking event. Bear in mind that people attending such an event *expect* to network. You will not immediately be viewed as an annoyance or imposition. However, you must make the contact beneficial to them, as they have many other options available to them.

Many job seekers have never attended such events as part of their careers. If you have never attended one, but plan to begin attending these events, some basic preparation is in order.

I worked with two excellent resources for information on attending such events: Lisa Wiley Parker, principal of Competitive Matrix, LLC, and Sherry Russell, who created a PowerPoint presentation specifically for our networking groups.

Before the event

First, equip yourself with business cards. They serve as the "currency" of such an event. Most attendees do not come prepared to tote away résumés. No need to panic! Vistaprint.com offers affordable business card services. Stores such as Staples and Office Depot can also help. No job seeker I have ever worked with has regretted investing in his or her own cards. They become a vital tool of the job acquisition process. Provide your contact information and a list of your skills and capabilities. Be creative about the display. Create something that will catch positive attention.

Research the event as much as possible prior to attending. Find out whatever you can about who may be attending. Sometimes, the sponsoring organization may have the list available. Call and inquire. This can assist you in targeting your contacts. You also will want to investigate the expected dress at the event. As tiresome as the axiom may seem, you only get one chance to make a first impression. You don't want it to be negative. Inappropriate attire will create an immediate bad impression.

Tip

Some events will require a fee to attend, a potential barrier for an unemployed candidate. Contact the group conducting the session ahead of time and volunteer to work at the event for a reduced or waived attendance fee. This also gives more insight into the attendee list.

For the novice networker, attending such an event with a friend or two can help. Prior to the event you can rehearse your introduction speeches together. Map out plans together for collecting information and follow-up. Friends may be able to help you locate desired contacts. If both of you are nervous, seeing someone in the same boat can relax you. I will never forget the first time I attended a chamber of commerce mixer during my injured worker placement days. My supervisor and mentor, Rich Brady, attended with me. It was also his first such event, and I cannot begin to tell you how much more relaxed

I felt when he compared his butterflies to those he felt attending his first dance in junior high school.

One warning about attending with someone you know: agree that once you arrive at the event, you will split up. Designate a time and place during the session to meet and compare notes. It can be easy to hang with another individual for comfort, but that's not the purpose of attending this event, and may get in the way of you making contacts.

Tip

If the idea of attending such an event truly overwhelms you, but you really see the need to do so, consider attending one or two just to observe. Watch how people "work the room." Get a sense of how concise their introduction is. See how they never linger too long with a particular individual. When someone approaches you, take similar notes about his or her presentation. This can help improve your own presentation.

At the event

Whether you have some designated target contacts or not, you should do some general mingling to become comfortable with the settings and surroundings. Sign in, get a name badge, and scope out the room.

One of the things Sherry Russell outlines for networkers in her presentation is how to read a group for potential acceptance of new conversation. Some of her pointers:

- If a pair of people is standing two feet or closer together, this means their conversation is most likely private. If more than two feet separate them, they are more likely to be receptive to someone joining the conversation.
- With a group of three or more members, see how open they are to the crowd. If they chat while focusing on the room, it's an open group. If they form more of a circle,

focusing their attention on each other, it's a closed group.

Some like to go right into their commercial after an introduction. Others like a little small talk regarding the event and some general information before delivering their information. A third popular option is to introduce yourself then immediately ask the other party about himself or herself. Initially, try the method that you are most comfortable with. If you are not having much success in getting your message across, then consider trying an alternate method. My natural inclination would be to invite the other party to talk first. People enjoy talking about themselves more anyway. The potential downfall can be that once some folks begin talking about themselves, they fail to stop. You cannot get a word in edgewise.

In tailoring your introduction speech for an event, keep in mind that everyone there will meet a significant number of people. You want to find ways to make yourself memorable. Possible ways to do so include:

- Provide details about a significant accomplishment. The more specific, the better the chance that you will be remembered.
- Add something humorous.
- Offer them a contact you know.
- Keep mental notes about significant accomplishments or characteristics you learn about people you meet. Jot these down on their cards. Mentioning such details in a follow-up contact will make a positive impression.
- Should you meet someone you had significantly targeted, start talking about something you know is important to him or her. This will make the most favorable first impression.

Avoid talking too long to one individual. Once everyone has exchanged their information, thank the others for their time, exchange business cards, and move on. If you "hang on" to someone too long, you will make a memorable impression, but not a positive one.

Only offer your business card if requested. Generally, once you request another's card, they will reciprocate. As you move on, jot down any notes regarding your conversation that will help you in any follow-up contact. Just as is the case with any other contact, how well you follow up will be critical to impressing the contact.

Do not hesitate to call someone back with potential leads that could be helpful to him or her. Also, when seeking to establish a good long-term relationship, try to connect four to six times per year.

So when you attend a networking function:

- Prepare ahead by researching the group and potential attendees. Script, practice, and rehearse your introduction speech.
- Once at the event, work the room according to your plan. Pay close attention to the body language of people you try to meet.
- As with any other contacts, follow-up is critical.

Chapter 10

Five Stories

Throughout my career, I have seen job seekers use a variety of networking techniques to land their dream job. Each has several factors in common. All were separated from jobs they greatly enjoyed. Each entered the job acquisition process with limited networking skills or understanding of the process, and they learned their skills along the way. Here are their stories.

Debbie

Debbie attended our workshop about two months after losing her job as communications manager for a large HMO. She had worked there for nearly three years. Prior to this, she had served as the director of publications at a college for over five years. Early in her career, Debbie was self-employed as a freelance graphic designer.

By the time she attended our seminar, she had already become frustrated with the classified ads and job boards. Compounding her dilemma was that in the two months of her unemployment, another unexpected event occurred: September 11, 2001. She had started to network with fellow professionals she knew in her field. This had established some leads. However, she often got little beyond information interviews. Much of the labor market appeared on hold.

Her separation was a "forced resignation," so she was not prepared for a long job search. She had not filed for unemployment, assuming she would be ineligible. Financial demands were becoming a problem for Debbie.

Tip

I advise anyone in such circumstance to file for benefits. Let your state's department of unemployment insurance determine your eligibility. Once again, do not assume a no!

Debbie looked at areas to expand her network. Even though she had not done freelance graphic design in over eight years, she began to draw up a list of old customers she'd worked with. She had two rationales for these calls. They could lead to additional contacts within the publishing field. Also, if money pressures continued, Debbie did not rule out doing freelance work to help pay some bills during the job acquisition process. Contacting old customers would help her determine how feasible this was.

Debbie breezed through her list of top former customers and received her share of leads. She followed up, producing some warm irons in the fire. No one appeared ready to make a hiring decision. Also, some short and quick freelance jobs were discussed. Further discussions developed into some small freelance jobs.

Since this was producing better results than job listings, Debbie decided to expand her efforts. She next went back to her old client lists and decided to contact customers she had done some work for, but not extensively. She could use the contact for the dual purpose of both career networking and prospecting for limited freelance work. Seeing the name of a particular client reminded her of a job she enjoyed very much. She was not even sure if the customer would remember her, but decided to take the chance and contact her. The customer very much remembered Debbie's work. They had a nice chat and Debbie explained her situation, indicating that she was open to a publishing firm or freelance work. The customer had no needs at the moment but they agreed to talk again toward the end of the calendar year.

Oddly, the next day the customer called Debbie back. After thinking about their conversation, she remembered a friend of hers who might have an interest in someone with Debbie's skills. She connected Debbie with the director of a family service agency. They were seeking a publications and public relations staff member. The problem they faced was that it would be a part-time job. Candidates had repeatedly balked at this. However, Debbie realized the hourly pay rate was quite good—forty-five dollars per hour. She described this as the first part-time opportunity she had ever come across in her field that provided professional-level pay. Other candidates also were concerned about the lack of benefits, but Debbie's family received benefits from her husband's job.

Debbie accepted the offer and loved the work. The part-time nature of the job allowed her to also satisfy an urge which the layoff had rekindled: freelance work. Her shortened workweek allowed time for her to continue doing some of the freelance work she'd developed through her contacts. She also hoped to pick up more projects on her own.

Key Points

- The most obvious lesson from this story is that Debbie never assumed a no. She made calls even when she was unsure a contact would remember her. This was the case with the contact who eventually landed her the job. One more subtle note: she always targeted decision makers. Thus, their referrals were also decision makers. This expedited the hiring decision process. The networks of decision makers often contain a higher percentage of fellow decision makers.

- Another big plus in Debbie's efforts came from the fact that, when contacting former customers, she was both job seeking as well as conducting research on her chances of freelancing. This put the focus of the contact more on advice and information as opposed to only seeking job openings. Thus, her contacts turned out to be more productive.

Ed

Ed spent most of his thirty-plus-year career in the apparel industry, eventually rising to the executive and vice president levels. He had experienced downsizing due to company reorganizations and bankruptcies twice before his most recent layoff. He had attempted to branch out to new areas during his previous job searches, to no success. Apparel still remained the area where he received the most interest and was most excited about, even though he still planned to consider other areas.

Similar to other manufacturing industries, most of the apparel companies in his area were in decline as a result of overseas competition. However, a new sports apparel company was growing at record rates. Ed firmly believed this company provided a career opportunity for him. An apparel company growing so rapidly could use someone with his industry expertise. Plus, unlike most other apparel companies in his area, this was growing. After three layoffs in the past seven years, this was most appealing to Ed.

Ed took every opportunity to research the company. He regularly attended network meetings at our center and joined other network groups. In addition to developing leads, he used these meetings to pick the brains of others on networking at this one particular company. Any story involving successfully finding a significant contact at a company provided him with new techniques.

He did not place all of his eggs in the one basket. He pursued other opportunities. Ed began carrying his résumé with him wherever he went. He even found a lead in the waiting room at a dentist's office. He had interviews with other companies, but no offers. Despite the delays, he never wavered in his interest in the sports apparel company. I am sure this helped ease his disappointment when he failed to turn up any offers. Finally, after seven months of networking, Ed got an interview with the company.

Ed recognized that the valuable feedback he had received in network groups helped him land the interview. So he next used the group to help prepare for the interview. After seven months of trying, there was little research he had not done about the company. He wanted guidance on handling one major aspect of the interview. The president and founder of the company was nearly twenty years younger than Ed. How much would this require Ed to adapt his normal interview style?

Our network groups do not always have speakers. Usually they consist of each member introducing himself or herself and what type of work he or she seeks. Each member follows this up with job acquisition plans for the upcoming weeks. At this meeting, Ed was one of the first to introduce himself. Once he stated that he sought feedback on interviewing with a younger boss, we may as well have had a speaker and topic. This theme dominated the session, and countless ideas and recommendations were exchanged.

A few weeks later, I received an amazing e-mail. Ed had been offered a ninety-day contract with the company as a consultant. He was told there was an excellent chance of a permanent position at the end of the contract. Sixty days later, an even better e-mail arrived from Ed. The company tore up Ed's ninety-day contract and started him as a full-time employee. I asked Ed to provide us with a synopsis of his efforts. His would be a great story for job seekers targeting a particular job or company. Here is his response:

Tom,

As per your request, here is my list of things you must do in a job search:

1. *Network.* The papers and Internet did not work for me. I got two interviews through the paper. None via the Internet.
2. *Stay focused.* Plan your attack daily. Don't ever give up!
3. *Target companies.* Research and contact people who can help you get in the door of your targeted organization. Be persistent. It took me seven months to get my first interview where I was hired.
4. *Talk to everybody.* I contacted as many people as I could to help me expand my network.
5. *Keep the faith and pray.*

Thanks for all of your help and please contact me if I can help you in any way.

Best regards,
Ed

A man of his word, Ed has happily provided referrals to countless people interested in his company. He also has linked our services to his church Web site. Given how much of a role networking played in landing his job, he hopes to provide future job seekers the same benefit.

Key Points

- Persistence! Many job seekers limit their follow-up with employers out of fear of imposing. Others assume one job rejection indicates a complete lack of interest. Some even fear that extensive follow-up might appear as "stalking" an employer. Rest assured, Ed never faced any potential stalking charges!

- Believe in the product of you! Remember, Ed believed that his knowledge and experience in the apparel industry could greatly benefit this upstart company. His conviction eventually proved to be correct. Sales representatives with a strong belief and confidence in their products or services think the same way. They know how their products or services can help a company's bottom line. When you identify a company you firmly believe your skills can benefit, think more like a sales representative. Do not give up at the first no. If you ask any successful sales representative if they regularly gave up on a customer after the first no, most will admit that if they had, they would never have found success in sales.

- Use your network for all phases of job acquisition. In addition to developing contacts within his target company, Ed also used the network forums to enhance his interview strategy.

Tip

Sadly, many job seekers overreact to a perceived initial rejection by an employer. If their résumé or application receives

**no reply or they interview with no resulting offer, many respond
by crossing that employer off their prospect list.**

An excellent Web site for any job seeker is Jobhunt.org. Two
contributors to the site are Kevin Donlin and David Perry, known as
the Guerilla Job Search Pros. They also have information on their
Web site GM4JH.com. On the topic of employer follow-up, they
remind job seekers of a marketing principle: It often takes seven
contacts before a customer decides to buy.

If you have a strong interest in a particular company, keep
approaching them! For example, if you have interviewed and not
received a job offer, write the employer a follow-up letter. Tell them
how excited you were about the prospect of the position, thus your
disappointment in not receiving an offer. Follow this by indicating
your continued interest in the company should similar openings occur
in the future. Donlin and Perry suggest inquiring if the employer has
any feedback which could help future interviews. This gives the
candidate another opportunity to demonstrate his or her high regard
for the company and opportunities it presents.

Companies are no different than people in the respect that they
enjoy hearing that people like them and want to work for them.
Given the costs of hiring, should another opening occur, many
would contact you about it rather than starting the hiring process
all over again. Additionally, one never knows what may happen
with the candidate receiving the first offer. He or she could accept
the position, then either before or after a start date receive an offer
more to his or her liking. Perhaps the candidate just does not work
out. Most companies restart the hiring process in lieu of contacting
candidates they have previously rejected. Your letter eliminates
this concern. I know of many cases where such a letter has led to a
subsequent offer.

John

In his senior year of college, John attended a job fair sponsored
by the school's placement office. He received an offer as a manager
trainee with a catalog showroom retail company, thus beginning

what would become a nineteen-year career with this outfit. His career moved quickly, rising to the store manager level ahead of the normal prescribed time period. He then earned positions in regional and corporate headquarters. During his tenure at corporate headquarters, the company came under chapter 11 bankruptcy. Rather than jump ship, as many long-time colleagues did, John stuck it out. He worked diligently on the reorganization plan, receiving several company awards and citations. The company eventually came out of bankruptcy.

Because several seasoned managers had left the company, many stores were being run by less-experienced managers. With the reorganization and bankruptcy work behind them, the corporate office felt John's experience would be best utilized as a district manager—with the caveat of returning to his home base. He spent several years covering one of their largest districts. Soon financial woes hit the company once again. This time, chapter 7 bankruptcy was filed, and the company ceased operations.

While there probably was not a retail function that he had not performed in his career, one thing became apparent: John had never trained for searching for a job. The last résumé he had written for anything other than an internal posting was in college. He sought the help of professional outplacement services, blasting résumés to major area retailers with mixed results. He found that few lateral positions opened to outside candidates at his level. The job clubs he attended through outplacement gave him ideas for network leads. He followed up on these, but never realized another network was available until it hit him full in the face.

While attending his son's Little League baseball practices, he recognized the name of a teammate his daughter used to babysit. He introduced himself to the boy's father, Dale, and they became bleacher buddies. Around their third meeting, Dale asked John what he did. Embarrassed, John explained that he was in a transition period. Turns out that Dale had just been through a layoff, had searched for several months, and had landed a job with a furniture distributor within the past few months. They spoke for quite a while about search techniques and the difficulties of the labor market. Dale offered to review John's résumé to get an idea of his skill sets in case he heard about anything.

A few weeks later at a game, John and Dale spoke again. Dale had given a copy of John's résumé to one of his customers, the owner of an office furniture outfit. The company was about to open a new division and realized they would need a president for this, as the increased level of responsibility would prove too much for the owner to handle along with his regular obligations. John followed up and began a series of interviews. Each one was more positive than the last, but their start-up date was pushed back a month. In the meantime a retail jewelry company showed interest in his résumé. They interviewed him and made him an offer. With no firm offer in hand from the office furniture firm, John had to accept.

Within the first two weeks at the jewelry company, John's experience with the company that ended up in chapter 7 opened his eyes. There was a huge volume of uncollected accounts receivables, obsolete inventory that had never been marked down, and an overstated balance sheet. He next discovered that the company's owner was seeking a buyer so he could retire in Florida.

Luckily, he received an offer from the office furniture company. He happily turned in his two-weeks notice and began a career in the office furniture business. As an added bonus, John quickly discovered that office furniture has a steadier year-round rate of sales than catalog showrooms. For the first time in nineteen years, mid-November through January would not require the twelve- to sixteen-hour days he endured with his previous job. He could actually look forward to enjoying the Christmas season.

Key Points

- Good network contacts can be found in all areas of your life. John now laughs about how his best offer came from networking at Little League baseball. Looking deeper at the situation, another reality emerged. He discovered how many other people have experienced job loss and faced the difficulties of the job acquisition process. Once job seekers begin expanding their personal networks, they often discover that many of their former colleagues, friends, and associates have experienced layoffs, downsizes, or unexpected periods of unemployment. Many times, they never realized their contacts have gone through this.

- Once anyone experiences a job loss and returns to work, he or she is very willing to assist a current job seeker. This serves as repayment to those who helped him or her. Whenever a re-employed customer of our program sends job openings to Steve Gallison, our director, he e-mails them to our full list under the title "pay it forward."

- Note that the job at the jewelry company came through a résumé posting. Therefore, most of the information John received about the company during the hiring process came from them. The company would not divulge the gravity of the situation on their own. Networked referrals often decrease, if not eliminate, the possibilities of this happening. An inside referral from a struggling company would not likely encourage a friend or former colleague to come on board a sinking ship.

Tip

While John regretted starting with the jewelry retailer to then leave within a month, he ultimately had to stay committed to his own financial and career priorities. When a job seeker develops numerous strong opportunities simultaneously, they likely may face multiple offers within a short period of time. If such a scenario happens, remember your first obligation remains to yourself.

Heather

Heather began her career as a writer and quickly moved into positions directing publications for national associations and resource centers. After struggling with integrity issues at her most recent position, she resigned. Focusing in on where she would like to work next, one factor became quite important. Her previous twelve years of work had required a ninety-minute daily commute into Washington, DC. Avoiding such drudgery was a primary focus of her next search. The headquarters of a large professional communications firm stood about ten minutes from her home. Thus, she identified this as a primary potential employer for her search and quickly discovered that they generally list any openings on their Web page. She began checking the site on a regular basis, but nothing in her skill set appeared for a while.

About three months into her search, she saw that a representative of the company, Lauren, was speaking at a professional association meeting. Heather maintained a passive membership in this association, but decided to attend this meeting in order to speak with Lauren. She and Heather met, discussed the company, and exchanged business cards.

Heather continued checking their Web site. Shortly thereafter, she spoke with a former coworker whose company did subcontract work for the desired company. Heather's colleague referred her to Lisa, her contact within the company. After hearing about Heather's background, Lisa referred her to Ann, the company's director of independent contracting. Ann immediately referred Heather to Elise, a human resource representative. Once they spoke, Elise requested her résumé and encouraged her to keep in touch. About two months later, a position listed on the company Web site caught Heather's eye. Even though she felt overqualified for the job, she followed up with the Elise to express her interest. Elise happened to be reviewing Heather's résumé for just that job. She had some of the same concern about Heather being overqualified, but was happy she had expressed interest. Two interviews followed with the HR department, the unit manager, and a potential coworker. The company generally agreed that she had more experience than the position would require, so no offer was extended at the time.

Despite the lapse of time, Heather remained impressed with everything she saw about the company throughout her dealings. Now that she had an established contact, she kept checking back with

Elise in HR. She told her nothing was new. Her continued contact was encouraged. Finally, she received a call for an interview with the HR manager and the vice president. In the process of scheduling this, she was informed that no specific opening existed.

Since she had never had an interview scheduled by the employer when no specific opening existed, Heather was curious about the content. She decided to contact Lauren, the woman from the association meeting. Lauren provided a wealth of information, and Heather went into the interview with lots of ideas and information. The VP and HR manager reiterated that no opening existed, but wanted to speak with her about leadership. They provided no more details and the interview ended.

Luckily, shortly after this meeting, Elise from the HR department contacted her. She told Heather that both interviewers had liked her and would be talking things over in hopes of finding a position for her. Heather continued to freelance over the next couple of months and regularly notified the company of relevant projects she worked on. Finally, about eight months after her initial contact, an offer was extended. She found out that they had brought her in to see if she would be a fit for a "situation that was not working out." While concluding Heather would be great in that position, they needed time to find a better situation for the employee in the position. Once this was worked out, they contacted Heather and made her the offer rather than advertising the position. Ironically, the very week all of this occurred, her husband received an abrupt layoff notice from his employer. This made Heather appreciate the way her new employer treated its employees.

Key Points

While this story has similarities to Ed's, Ed's eventual employer was his primary target. Heather had a high priority with this employer while keeping several additional irons in the fire. She never stopped networking her company sources throughout the entire duration. Many job seekers use a network lead to get their foot in the door and discontinue once an internal contact is established. Like Ed, this allowed Heather to impress multiple employees and continuously demonstrate her interest.

Too often job seekers discontinue working with a contact when immediate results fail to happen. They must keep in mind that other people's time frames and priorities differ from theirs. Do not assume that a contact's failure to deliver information in a time frame suitable to you means he or she cannot or does not want to help. The time lapses in Heather's story might have frustrated other seekers to give up on the company, but she held firm.

She used her contacts to discuss new information and openings. This allowed her to get feedback on her potential candidacy when she saw openings. She also could address the "overqualified" concern for the one position enough to at least get an interview. Many job seekers view such an interview as a waste of time, because no offer resulted. Obviously, the company determined they liked her, and was in search of a more suitable position for her talents. Had she not received her initial interview, the results may have been very different.

Greg

Greg's story begins with an illustration about how a situation that might appear perfect for establishing contacts can hit some unforeseen stumbling blocks. For several years, Greg ran a successful branch of a staffing company. His office worked with most of the top employers in his community. A larger, national staffing firm purchased Greg's company. The new owners opted to move their own personnel into most of the offices they acquired rather than retain existing personnel, so Greg lost his job.

One would assume that with the contacts he had developed running a staffing agency, Greg would have no trouble landing a new job. Unfortunately, when he reached the management level at his firm, company policy required him to sign a non-compete clause. This prohibited him from accepting employment with any former client for one year after separation. He quickly learned that the acquiring agency planned to enforce the clause.

Over my years in career services, I have seen countless individuals use an unexpected job loss as an opportunity for self-reflection. Many begin careers, work hard, and move up the promotional chain. As they do so, they add financial responsibilities commensurate with their growing income level. Sometimes the changes in responsibility that accompany moving up the ladder pull a worker further away from the aspects of the job or career that drew them to that occupation in the first place. Or, maybe he or she based his or her original job or career choice more on income potential than on passion for the work. Whatever the reason, he or she finds himself or herself working every day in a job that does not fulfill him or her in the way he or she hoped or as much as an earlier job once had. However, his or her accrued financial responsibilities make any career change out of the question.

Greg began such a self-examination. While he had enjoyed managing his staffing firm and its success, he realized that if he ranked where most of his fulfillment came from, the job would easily fall behind his family and faith. While ranking things honestly, he admitted that his passion for the game of lacrosse also rated higher than many of his career successes. He played while attending a local university, and after graduation he continued to play the sport. He fed his passion for lacrosse by developing into a top-notch referee on high school, college, and international levels. On more than one occasion, he was chosen to referee the international championships.

Having known many of his fellow lacrosse referees for years, Greg informed them of his employment status. The schedule chairman made certain he assigned Greg as many games as possible to ease income concerns a bit. While spending many hours on the lacrosse field, Greg often spoke with his old coach at his alma mater. The coach informed him that the school's athletic department planned to hire a development officer. The more Greg thought about this opportunity, the more he realized how perfectly that met his career desires. He could work for the university he loved, and benefit student athletes with backgrounds similar to his own.

Despite having no prior university-level development experience, Greg was able to meet the search committee based on the recommendation of the lacrosse coach. However, they selected another candidate with previous experience in athletic department development at another university. The rejection hurt, but did not diminish the passion he felt for the job possibility. With the support of his family, Greg approached the athletic director with an offer to hire him on a part-time basis for one year. He offered the provision that if he doubled his earning goals, he would attain full-time status in one year. The athletic director gave him the chance.

Greg more than doubled his earning goal and became a full-time employee at the university. Two factors played a major part in this. First, he found the sales aspect of development work amazingly easy due to his strong commitment to the university and sports, as an alumnus and former student athlete. Selling something he believed in so deeply came naturally. Second was what his own job search had taught him; how important networking is. While he had none of university-level development experience others in the department had, having played there he still knew many associated athletes from both his playing days and subsequent refereeing work. He had contacts and would not hesitate to use them. Searching for a new career taught him to never talk himself out of a contact.

Greg's continued success in his role has led the university to promote him to the position of assistant athletic director, development. Recognizing one of the keys to his success, he works with the university career center to sponsor an annual career information networking fair. Unlike traditional job fairs, the format will bring alumni and university friends into a forum where students can meet them to learn about their careers. This will allow the students to begin establishing networks of their own.

Key Points

As a true novice networker, the willingness of his contacts to help him amazed Greg. Remember, since his initial purpose was career exploration, his contacts focused on seeking information. He wanted to explore options on how he could carve a new career for himself in athletics. People will respond much more enthusiastically to contacts seeking their expertise. Additionally, their expertise most likely extends well beyond their place of employment. Even when someone has a true desire to help, when a call focuses only on potential job openings, the receiver can only help if any appropriate openings exist. When you seek someone's professional opinion on career direction, you open the door to any of their knowledge of possibilities. Trust that if you make a positive impression on the call, you will also find out about any openings at their company.

Realistically, without any of university development experience, Greg never would have gotten in front of the search committee without the recommendation of a primary network contact—his former coach. Even though the meeting did not result in an initial job offer, he impressed the athletic director enough to accept Greg's trial proposal.

Once Greg discovered that his dream job actually existed, he refused to allow the initial turndown to deter him. He offered the university a low-risk opportunity to prove himself. He had the confidence that his passion and commitment to the university would produce results strong enough to gain full-time status.

Tip

This is far from the first time I have seen a job seeker offer a "low cost, low risk" option to an employer to get their foot in the door and prove themselves. Offers have involved things ranging from starting on contract, with no benefits, or quarterly status reviews toward goals. In each case the job seeker felt passionate about the opportunity and initiated the offer. If you see an opportunity you want badly enough and know you can deliver, what do you have to lose by making such an offer?

Chapter 11

After Your Job Offer

No matter how long the job acquisition period, few things feel as exhilarating as receiving and accepting a job offer. The weight of the world has definitely lifted off your shoulders.

Tip

Before I address a way to give your network the good news and thank them, the résumé writer in me must make a standard proclamation. I realize that after revising, editing, posting, and mailing so many of them during your job acquisition period, your résumé is probably the last thing you want to look at right now. However, you should immediately put your new job onto the résumé. This way, you can keep a much better running record of the projects worked on and achievements you'll need to document. Should you need to produce it again—hopefully for a promotion—you have it ready immediately.

That said, once you have accepted your offer, you will feel a great sense of appreciation for all the individuals who aided your search in any form. I received a wonderful example of what one new hire sent to the network of people who assisted his transition. Luckily, he gave me permission to use his letter. The experiences he describes below are not unusual. Here is the letter:

Dear Friends:

I have just accepted a job offer with the United States government. The agency wishes to put my communications skills to good use and I'll also receive a significant pay raise. Monday is my start date.

First, I want to thank all of you for your never-ending support to my wife, children, and me. I am humbled by all those who provided me with blunt advice and counsel that was hard to hear, but necessary to understand. Many of you shared your wisdom. You also shared the difficulties and personal trauma of being suddenly unemployed, and what it took to establish your personal momentum. These were powerful and convincing lessons that assisted my family and me. Thank you for being honest and sharing such a personal side of yourselves.

It is impossible to list all the help that was rendered. So many wrote letters, made phone calls, or convinced others I deserved a "look" that a list would take days to complete. Your résumé reviews and general encouragement sustained my family and me.

What really astounds me were the relative and complete strangers who provided considerable assistance based solely on the recommendations of friends or former coworkers. I recently had an occurrence where a professional spent three hours helping me prepare for an interview. This person knew who I was, but was under no obligation to take so much of his valuable time to get me ready. But all it took was a phone call from someone in my network, and he quickly offered me his services the following morning. I could offer multiple examples of people providing extraordinary assistance. Again, friends came to my assistance, and provided me with connections necessary to gain the upper hand.

I often wondered what form this letter would take when I found work. What I hoped and prayed for was a position that would allow me to support my family. I also prayed for a position I would enjoy and take pride in. I feel I have secured those qualities with my new position. My new colleagues are dignified, seasoned professionals. I am honored to join their team.

It is strange to say that this has been a positive event. It was positive because of those who took the time to help us. I will never look at unemployment the same way, and my door will always be open to those in need of employment assistance. My wife and I plan to immediately provide financial assistance to someone who is out of work and struggling financially, and stay with that person and their family until they recover. We will do this in the name of those who helped us. I have contacted the unemployment office asking for a family in need.

We will have a party in the next couple of weeks to thank you personally. God bless you all and God bless America.

This letter speaks volumes about the entire networking process. Obviously, prior to this layoff the author had little to no idea how many people had experienced a job loss. Learning from their experiences proved as valuable as contacts. He clearly discovered how a little connection can open doors previously closed. Finally, he saw how many people are willing to offer aid to a job seeker. So many people have walked many miles in those shoes. They would love the opportunity to shorten somebody else's walk. They just need to be asked.

I am sure all those who received his letter were impressed with his gratitude. Once you get your offer, give all who have aided your search the same opportunity. It's very easy if you've set up an e-mail list during your search.

Those of us who make a career of assisting people in job acquisition recognize the degree to which one's job impacts his or her entire life and self-esteem. Being any part of helping someone improve his or her life can be extremely rewarding, especially when you receive acknowledgement for it. We remember the Steve Gallison quote about "cashing a psychic check" each time a customer finds his or her next job. Give your friends and contacts a chance to experience that feeling through your good news.

Finally, after your ordeal, just like our author, give yourself the chance to experience such feeling. Always keep your door open to a job seeker. This is how you can repay those who helped you.

I truly hope that you have found this book beneficial. I want to help as many job seekers as possible avoid conducting job searches with their dominant hand tied behind their back. If you fail or choose not to network, you will adopt inferior job search strategies. More than just providing reluctant networkers with strategies, I want to challenge the impediments you place on yourself.

If your barrier stems from a lack of understanding of how and why networking plays such a critical role in hiring decisions, hopefully you now see more clearly the steps an employer takes in making hiring decisions. Employers value referrals from people they know and trust because this method has proven so successful in the past. Also, employers face large costs in terms of dollars and staff time when advertising job openings. With this in mind, you can appreciate more why they choose advertising the opening as a last resort.

Additionally, seeing the many ways networking can make you a better informed and prepared candidate, you will now utilize this resource more extensively. You may also realize that your lack of a complete understanding of how the entire labor market works has made you adopt a limited strategy in your own job search.

If fear holds you back, examining the common networking misconceptions should challenge you to consider exactly what about networking you actually fear. Once you have a better understanding of this, you can take stronger steps to overcome the fears.

Commit yourself to daily steps outlined in chapter 7 as part of the strategies recommended in developing and making contacts. Should you want to tackle networking events, chapter 9 provided guidelines for attending those situations with an action plan.

I want to close by addressing the individual stories referenced throughout the book. Each case cited shares a common trait. None of the individuals had ever attempted such a strategy in his or her job search before. These people committed themselves to improving the networking level in their job acquisition process with excellent results. Having worked with so many similar people and seeing my own growth, I can assure you that networking is a skill that anyone can continuously improve and master. You just need to commit to doing so, analyze and overcome your fears and misperceptions, and start reaching out.

Notes

1. Richard N. Bolles, *What Color Is Your Parachute* (10 Speed Press, 2005), 38.
2. Penelope Trunk, *Brazen Careerist: The New Rules for Success* (Warner Business Books, 2007), 45.
3. Dale Carnegie, *How to Win Friends and Influence People* (Pocket Books, 1936), 31.
4. Jeffery Gitomer, *The Sales Bible: The Ultimate Sales Resource* (Collins, 2008), 65.
5. Orville Pierson, *The Unwritten Rules of a Highly Effective Job Search* (McGraw Hill, 2006), 5.
6. Kathryn Kraemer Troutman, *Ten Steps to a Federal Job* (The Resume Place, 2002), 23.
7. Kathryn Kraemer Troutman, *Ten Steps to a Federal Job* (The Resume Place, 2002), 29.
8. Kathryn Kraemer Troutman, *Ten Steps to a Federal Job* (The Resume Place, 2002), 59.
9. Kathryn Kraemer Troutman, *Ten Steps to a Federal Job* (The Resume Place, 2002), 71.